The Great Love

We Came Here as Teachers of Love And Got Enrolled in the School of Fear

by Paul Six and Norman Hawker

Cover art by Norman Hawker

©2005 by Paul Six and Norman Hawker. All rights reserved.

ISBN 1-4116-3009-2

This book is available at:
www.lulu.com/content/121169

To Orelia and Monti

I have just met you and yet I know you are angels in disguise and I would like to know more about you

May The Great Love Shine through you and light up your world

www.PaulSix.com
PaulSix2000@yahoo.com

all the best,

Paul Six

604 726 5030

Preface

At the age of 33, I skipped out on a life as a successful businessman and spent the next seven years immersed in a metaphysical study of invisible energies, a study that captured my interest more than anything in the visible world. I had grown up with the mind of a skeptic and questioned almost everything presented to me. I am grateful, though, that I had the childhood conditioning I did because much of the information I took in during this period I perceived as nonsense. I crossed paths with a colorful cast of characters in the metaphysical community, all claiming to know the truth, yet many of them impressed me as charlatans.

I soon realized that no matter what I said or did, some people would perhaps view me as an imposter as well. To counter this risk I committed to a mastery of my subject, reading more than a thousand books on astrology, philosophy, psychology and religion. I did this all on my own without any outside motivation to push me forward. I began to offer intuitive readings and more and more people came to see me. I had no academic credentials to support my practice, yet my clients never questioned this. They saw that I had a gift for this work, a talent that I myself cannot completely explain.

In 1981 my colleague Norman Hawker and I created and conducted a series of workshops entitled Identity Development. We both felt that the information astrology provided would be more meaningful and useful if it were simplified. That is exactly what we did—we stripped the astrological body of knowledge down to the bare bones and focused on its underlying structure. Then we presented it in a new form, dressed in modern clothes and communicated in ordinary language. Over the next two decades Identity Development and the private consultations that I gave in association with it reached over 15,000 people in twelve countries.

When I began collaborating with Norman Hawker again at the end of 2004, I had just completed an intensive five-month period studying western religions. I wanted to understand how people came to form the opinions that they held about the nature of reality and the elusive entity we refer to as the truth. Although millions of people pursue spirituality in ways that are off the beaten path, I knew that the majority honored the religious tradition in which they were raised and tended not to challenge these beliefs.

What impressed me most was the gap between western religious teachings and the way those who proclaimed to follow these teachings actually lived their lives. The words of wisdom espoused by these religions were revered in theory, yet most of those who claimed to be disciples showed a disdain for the life of voluntary simplicity and humble devotion these religions advocated.

Working in Asia, I experienced a completely different culture than the one I knew in the United States. In Asia people feel more of a connection with one another and place more importance on the greater good and collective values. In America intense individualism and competition seem to be the standards most people adhere to, creating an imbalance within the society. Typically masculine, aggressive tactics prevail, even among the female of the species.

The glorification of masculine dominance, a form of worship one might have thought had met its final nemesis with the fall of Nazi Germany, has remained intact, though it might not appear to be as extreme. The intent to have success at any price has led to a mindset that downplays the nurturing capacities associated with the feminine in favor of the macho approach to engulf and devour.

I have been astonished in my twenty-four years as a spiritual teacher that most Americans that I encountered, especially men, could not understand someone who was coming from love instead of a desire for money, sex and power. They could not fathom how someone could be so devoted to the work that they were doing without focusing on any specific reward. It showed me that masculine materialistic values rule the American mind.

The book you are about to read has been written as a reminder that the true nature of a human being is love, that the spirit we refer to as 'God' is love, that love is the one absolute, and that love is what keeps us from destroying ourselves. Violence is evidence of the presence of pain and love is its healing agent. When meeting anger with love, as in turning the other cheek, a human being shows great strength.

Hostility begins once an 'us against them' dynamic is created. One group assumes the right to tell another what to do, thus declaring superiority over them. In turn, a contest ensues in which the opposing groups go to war to prove who has God on their side, as if God could be against God. Fighting fire with fire only perpetuates the pain of conflict, all too often indefinitely. This is how the world becomes artificially polarized and how the division continues to widen as each group strikes back at the other. The separation is an illusion that has existed for as long as we know.

In my own life I have come to understand that what I perceive happening around me actually tells me about myself. What I have sent out is what the world reflects back to me, as if it were a mirror. While on the physical level it may not be so apparent, on the energetic level it is clear to me that I am the origin of all that I attract into my life. This book has been written to share this awareness. The book points to a potential future that may sound as if it is pure idealism. To those who reject the idea that they are accountable for their experiences, and who continue to make the consequence of their actions someone else's responsibility, the messages conveyed may seem romantic and impractical. For me, however, what is being said here is more real than what is commonly held to be the truth.

The first step towards transforming any part of a life that is based in fear is to endorse the idea that the most powerful force in existence is love. As the saying goes, it conquers all. We can try to limit the power of love and say it is something personal and special. We can misinterpret it and make it another game for the ego to play. We will forever lose that game, however, until we restore love to its rightful place in the scheme of things. Love will uplift us all once we make it our highest priority and the ultimate conclusion as to the meaning of life on earth. Then, notwithstanding all of our so-called realistic attitudes and our intellectual arguments, we will see that it is the energy of love that can create peace on earth, and it is the only energy that ever could.

Paul Six

My role in collaborating with Paul has been to focus on the underlying structure of ancient wisdom and find a way to present its essence simply, without flourish. In 1981 we invented a three-dimensional astrological horoscope with a spinning color wheel and colored pieces for the planets. We created a seminar series that taught the principles behind the astrological signs, planets and houses so that participants could interpret their own chart and better remember its meaning.

Over the years since then, I saw a tendency for people to define themselves as their egocentric personality. I felt that the world needed all of us to expand beyond our egos so that the love that we truly are could come through. I longed to find a way to convey a message that every one of us is all of it.

I knew that astrology held profound wisdom about the nature of the human experience and the core issues every person faces. Without abandoning the wisdom I had learned, I sought to depersonalize it. Rather than focus on a finite sense of self, I wanted to offer an expansive self concept that is more universal. To that end, Paul and I have written the story you are about to read.

While our light-hearted fable may seem simple at first, it is based on a body of knowledge that has a great deal of substance. Please give the characters in this story a chance to reach your place of inner knowing. They want to know if the Great Love inside you can come out and play!

Norman Hawker

Table of Contents

INTRODUCTION
Teachers of Love 1

LESSON ONE
BUD - "I need to get my way" 9
From Egotism to Authenticity

LESSON TWO
MOLLY - "I need more stuff" 21
From Greed to Gratitude

LESSON THREE
STEVEN - "I need to know more" 29
From Superficiality to Awareness

LESSON FOUR
MARJORIE - "I need to protect myself" 35
From Insecurity to Trust

LESSON FIVE
MAX - "I need to be somebody" 43
From Pride to Generosity

LESSON SIX
AGNES - "I need to be helpful" 49
From Criticism to Humility

LESSON SEVEN
BRETT - "I need to be with someone" 57
From Dependency to Respect

LESSON EIGHT
AURORA - "I need to be fulfilled" 63
From Insatiability to Passion

LESSON NINE
LANCE - "I need to be right" 71
From Arrogance to Wisdom

LESSON TEN
KATHERINE - "I need to prove myself" 81
From Callousness to Integrity

LESSON ELEVEN
MORGAN - "I need to be different" 87
From Rebelliousness to Freedom

LESSON TWELVE
CRYSTAL - "I need to be happy" 95
From Escapism to Transcendence

INTRODUCTION

Teachers of Love

When we look into the eyes of an infant we see nothing but pure love. Inevitably, our faces light up with a smile that comes from deep within us.

The baby is teaching us about love, showing us what love looks like and more importantly what it feels like. The love that pours out from the baby makes everything lighter, softer and more beautiful.

A newborn baby models a consciousness that knows no fear and has no unmet needs. The baby neither regrets the past nor dreads the future. It possesses, instead, a complete acceptance of the present.

How many of us are currently living in this state of consciousness? Is there anything we can do to recapture it? How did we lose our childhood innocence and sense of wonder? Perhaps the answers can be explained by examining the human ego.

When we separate from the world and from other human beings, when we see everything and everyone as being external to us, we are operating through ego. Ego feels special, sounds boastful and acts superior. Still, beneath the façade, ego is hurting from insecurity.

The ego decides that parts of life are desirable and parts of life are not. It divides experience and labels one part good and one part bad. Focusing solely on what we like or dislike only brings unhappiness. We tend to forget that we are here to witness the dance of life and learn from it, rather than sit in judgment of it.

The ego does have a vital function. It helps us to integrate our energies and channel them effectively. A certain amount of ego is necessary so that we can go beyond the ordinary and achieve excellence in our individual efforts.

Ego works against us, however, if we believe we are better than others and condemn anyone who does not agree. Ego covers up our essence with a wall of protection. It is fear that builds that wall, and it is love that can tear it down so that we can express who we truly are. We have a choice to reprogram our fearful responses to life by replacing them with loving ones. If this becomes our intention and we nourish our mind with loving thoughts, we can shine a light into the darkness and make the world a better place simply by being in it.

Encounters with the Master

This book examines the ways in which we have moved from love to fear. It explores the possibilities for returning to our original state of purity, where the present moment is met with a generous reception and our response is a gift of love.

The book presents these ideas in the form of a fable. In the story, twelve students hear about a sage named Master Wiseheart. The Master is sharing his wisdom with all those who visit him in his yurt, just outside of town. One by one, the students go to see the wise man to discuss specific issues that are troubling them. One by one, they experience a shift in consciousness in his presence. The Master teaches the students to trust the life process and let the world be. He tells them that this is the way to access the Great Love, an enormously loving energy that can flow through their being and raise the vibrations wherever they are.

The first one to meet the Master was Bud. Our story begins with him.

Hi!

Name's Bud.

I want to tell you my part of an amazing story. I have gone through such a transformation.

Do you have some time? I really want to get into this.

I feel as if I have come full circle. Way back, before I remember, I was comfortable resting in my mother's womb. I was preparing to be born.

Suddenly I was evicted. An eruption took place and I came into this world. I was yanked, held upside down and slapped. It was a jolting experience!

I could feel something unhealthy about this place I was in. Later, I learned it was unhealthy because it was filled with people who were sick. It was called a hospital. I began to contract in that place, as if already I was beginning to lose a little bit of who I was.

Who am I? Well, that's a really important question! I'm beginning to realize that who I am really, is a part of the Great

Love. And that's who I was when I came into this world—a teacher of love.

You know how adults light up when they see a baby's face? They look into those innocent eyes and they see nothing but pure, unadulterated love. And how many parents have said that they learned so much from their children? That's what I mean by 'a teacher of love.'

The world turned out to be like a school of fear, though—everybody telling you what to watch out for and what not to do. Despite how it sounds, the school of fear is not a bad place. It's a testing ground for us to learn how to share our love. The school of fear will show you how constant your love actually is. It will test you in a way that makes your love grow stronger, so strong that it can overcome fear forever.

Anyway, back to the story. For the first few years of my life I tried to remain in the peaceful place that I was in prior to my birth. As I grew older it became harder to stay there.

When I entered the world I had no concept of being separate from anything around me. It wasn't long before I began to realize that other people were other people, and I didn't like it! I wanted to be the only one. I wanted it to be all about me.

I began to feel separate and apart from everything. Now, instead of sensing how I was connected to my surroundings, I perceived the people around me in opposition to almost all the things I wanted to do.

They kept saying:

Don't do that!
Don't touch that!
Don't say that!

Every time I asserted my independence, my well intentioned, protective parents stopped the flow of my energy. They would tell me I didn't know what I was doing. For a long time I lacked the understanding as to why they treated me this way. Later I realized that they were afraid I would go too far too fast and take on more than I could handle. And they were right—I would have!

I like to meet the world head on. I tell my truth in the moment. I don't listen too much to what others have to say.

My parents would grow angry because of disappointments and frustrations in their own lives that had little to do with me. Life seldom worked out the way they wanted it to, and at times they lost heart. It's not that my parents lacked faith, but faith kind of took a back seat when day-to-day concerns became more pressing.

I was unable to care for myself back then so I played along. I believed that love would triumph over anything, yet my parents had a different experience. They had been in the school of fear for a long time and I'm not sure they ever graduated.

As the school of fear taught me to value strength and avoid any show of weakness, I learned to be competitive. I felt small, so I acted big. I learned to behave as if I thought I was better and more entitled than anyone who crossed my path. I was just getting started and I was pretty much in the dark about how the game of life can be played successfully. So I covered up my fears with a false bravado. I guess some people would call it egotism. I behaved as if the sun in the sky rose and set just for me.

My parents kept telling me one thing I really did not want to hear. They told me that if I wanted to succeed in the world, I could not always have my way. I grew increasingly unhappy because more and more it seemed as if I could hardly ever get my way. In school I had to learn what the teachers insisted I learn. If I wanted to make friends with my schoolmates, I felt pressured to be more like them and think the way they did. My parents took me to church every Sunday and told me to believe whatever the church said was the truth.

I felt at times that the demands life placed on me were excessive and that I was simply not good enough. I grew confused. On the one hand, I wanted to succeed in the world. On the other hand, I wanted to change the world so that I could do life my way.

Every time I attempted to change things to my liking, however, I fell flat on my face.

Not long ago my friends and I met someone we'll never forget. We had some experiences that I can only describe as amazing.

It was in the presence of a sage, a man named Master Wiseheart, that I finally understood why I kept encountering challenging experiences. The challenges were teaching me not to tamper with the world. I mean, it sure has been here a lot longer than I have! I decided I was not on earth to change the world but to add something to it, something that would help others improve their lives. As their lives improved, the world would change for the better in the process. It was then that I understood how my life lessons were offering me the wisdom and helping me gain the strength to accomplish my task. That is when I stopped blaming the world or anyone in it for the unhappiness I felt. Then and there, in the Master's tent, I made up my mind that it was up to me to share the love in my heart and allow nothing to deter me from this purpose.

Somewhere along the way, my view had become clouded. I had closed my heart because I thought life was happening to me. My story is about how I learned to open my heart again and remember that I am the one happening to life. As I moved out of a black hole of fear and returned to my natural state of love, I realized that all that I see is not separate from me. That is the illusion. The truth is, all that I see says a lot about me.

This is when I had a shift in consciousness. I could actually experience myself as a part of all that is—the earth and the sky and the stars—everything in the universe. I saw that I was an expression of the Great Love. Wow! That's big! Still, I knew I had a long way to go and a lot of work to do before I could be a real star.

Instead of moving into fear when things do not unfold the way I want them to, I now see that I can express a more authentic self that doesn't depend on getting what I want. I can work with what I have without complaining—and that's better for everybody.

I now know in my heart that the way for me to be real is to always come from love. When I learn to trust the life process and let the world be, the purity of my loving self flows through *my being. Then I can focus on my part rather than be distracted by what everyone else is doing. The greatest gift I can offer to others is to simply be myself.*

LESSON ONE

BUD – "I need to get my way"

Bud's initial reactions to life were fearful ones. Instead of connecting to the flow of life, Bud was separating from everything around him and seeing society as a competitive struggle for survival. The result was that all he had left was egotism to sustain his existence. He kept thinking his separate ego was who he was—and all that he was—instead of identifying with the one undivided consciousness that unites us all.

Time and again the same lesson kept repeating as if a voice from somewhere were reminding Bud, "Life on earth is not just about you. It is not just about any single individual. It is about all of us."

These reminders gave Bud another opportunity to move into a more inclusive frame of mind and expand his sense of self. Still, Bud could not let go of the idea that he was his ego. He continued to view all of the attitudes and opinions and judgments that he identified as his own as the truest things about him. After all, it was his ego that provided him with the motivation to keep going and continue to make an effort. It was his ego that enabled him to recover from defeat and begin again. It was his ego that inspired him to surpass previous accomplishments.

On the other hand, Bud's ego was the source of his sense of separation.

From Egotism to Authenticity

Bud heard from a fellow student that there was a wise man living in a yurt on the outskirts of town dispensing advice without charging for it. Bud thought, 'why don't I go check this guy out?'

Bud had no trouble finding the round tent in the woods. He knocked on the door and heard a voice inviting him inside. As he stepped into the circular room, he saw a man sitting in the middle of the floor in a lotus position. Bud knew right away that it was the Master.

"Welcome," said Master Wiseheart. "What can I do for you today?"

The Master's small frame was dressed simply in a long red robe. His head was shaven. He had a kindly face and a peaceful vibe about him.

Bud came right down to the issue that was troubling him. "I want to do things my way, but the world keeps interfering with me. It seems I hardly ever get my way,"

"What makes you think you are not getting your way?" asked the wise man.

"I don't like how things turn out. I'm always arguing with what's happening and want it to be different. Why am I this way? Others say you are a wise man. Surely you have the answer."

The wise man remained silent for a few moments. As Bud looked into his eyes he was struck by how remarkably intense they were, and yet they were not threatening. Bud felt very much at ease in his presence.

Finally Master Wiseheart spoke. "The life you are living is based on a false belief. This false belief began with Adam and Eve. According to the biblical story, Adam and Eve originally lived in a blissful state of unity. They were not afraid of anything, saw no need to protect themselves and felt no need to prove their worth. On the other hand, Adam and Eve were unaware that everything was perfect. They were like fishes in the sea who do not know the ocean because the ocean is all there is."

"If everything was perfect, why did they leave?" asked Bud.

"They were tempted by the prospect of making their own choices and they ate the sour apple."

"The sour apple? What is that?"

"The sour apple of duality. Once they ate it, everything changed. Instead of experiencing unity, they saw a world filled with opposites: right and wrong, good and bad, you and me, now and then. Suddenly, Adam and Eve each started to believe they were separate and alone in this world, and based on this false belief they began to make choices that denied the truth of who they were—and who we all are."

"Well who are we?" asked Bud.

"Each of us is a significant part of a magnificent perfection."

"Why isn't the world perfect then?"

"If the only option available is to express God-like perfection," replied the Master, "then there is no choice and there is no free will. We do have a choice, and most of us are choosing to be ruled by our independent ego rather than by our universal self.

Adam and Eve were the first ones to make this choice, and their descendents have been doing the same ever since."

"Why would people choose to let ego rule their life?" inquired Bud.

"They choose to follow their ego," answered Master Wiseheart, "because of a false belief that the source of life and thus the cause of life is something external. This belief leaves them feeling empty inside, and it is an emptiness that can never be filled. They fail to realize that the true cause of each person's life is an internal source of light and love."

"You mean to say," asked Bud, "that the creation of my life originates from me?"

"Yes. The light that created the physical universe is the same light that created you, Bud. Your purpose in life, like everyone's, is to reconnect with the true source of being and reunite with the rest of creation."

"How do I do that?"

"You already have the answer," said the wise one. "The answer is in your heart. It is the heart pumping your life essence throughout your body that transmits the truth of who you are to all your cells. It is the awareness of what is in your heart that enables you to remember what you came here to do."

"Sometimes I do hear what my heart is saying but my mind keeps telling me something else," Bud complained.

"Be sure your head is in line with your heart," said the Master. "Thoughts are things, and they are very powerful. If your heart and your mind make joint decisions, your choices will be wise ones."

"What do you mean when you say thoughts are things?" Bud asked.

"Our thoughts are composed of energies that eventually become solid enough to be seen as real," the Master explained. "Our thoughts are like 'Coming Attractions,' a preview of our future. The more you focus on any idea, the more likely it is to materialize."

"You make everything sound so simple," Bud replied. "Look at all the terrible things that happen in the world, often to people who are innocent. I do not believe that most of these people wanted to undergo these negative experiences. Can you explain this?"

The wise man's response surprised Bud. "No one has the answer as to why goodhearted souls suffer unfortunate, even horrible, fates. Life may contain random elements of danger; however, constantly dwelling on this possibility will only serve to bring the potential danger closer and make it more real. Perhaps that is why some of us meet fates that do not appear justified."

"Is there anything we can do to avoid danger?" Bud asked.

"If we have enormous self love and a deep sense of caring," Master Wiseheart replied, "that is our best insurance against harm coming to us. We are most likely to experience a peaceful world when we have peace in our hearts, even if conflict and strife are still around us. To have peace, we must first be it."

"But how can I be at peace when almost everything around me is at war?" Bud protested.

"You have to tap into the Great Love," said the Master.

"The Great Love? What is that?"

"It is a love that is pure," the Master answered, "a love that has no expectations, no attachments, and no limits. It allows everything to be the way it is without trying to change it. It is a love that supports each and every expression."

"What is my relationship to the Great Love?" Bud asked the Master.

"It is your true self, buried alive inside you, and it wants to come out. It is up to you to release it."

"How would I do that?"

"For you to do so, you would first have to break through the barrier of the ego. Your ego, Bud, attempts to restrict the light inside from shining through. It also blocks any incoming information that it does not wish to absorb. While at times this is helpful in warding off overstimulation, there is a downside to this process."

"What's the downside?" Bud asked.

"You stay focused on what you have been taught to believe is plausible," said the Master, "and this determines what you see in the world as well as how you perceive it. Your upbringing and education have directed you to expect reality to show up in a certain way and your mind tenaciously maintains that worldview."

"I don't want my life to be a product of anyone else's imagination," said Bud. "I want my life to be my own creation, my own discovery."

"It certainly can be, Bud, because it is your thinking that determines the way you perceive the world, and your thinking can be changed. You may be looking at the same world as everyone around you, yet you are seeing it through your own unique filter. You would have no recognition of qualities you perceive in the world if those qualities weren't lit up inside of you. That is why you give your attention to them. This is the connection between what you see and what you are. In a sense, every perception you have tells you something more about yourself."

"Are you saying that there really is no world and that there is only perception?" asked Bud.

"There is a world," said Master Wiseheart, "a world all of us have created through our thoughts, our feelings and our actions. Your experience of that world, however, is yours alone. No other person is responsible for how you see, hear, taste, touch and smell. Essentially, every thought you have about life is subjective. It is only because you were trained to see what others have seen, so that you could be on the same page as the rest of society, that any of your perceptions could be considered objective. This training is necessary to some degree if you wish to be a participant in that society, yet it is not natural."

Bud contemplated the wise man's teaching. "What you are telling me is that I see life in my own way. Well, seeing life my own way is what makes me an individual."

"You are an individual," said the Master. "Let no one take that away from you. You are capable as well of being an embodiment of the Great Love."

"What is preventing me from opening up to the Great Love?"

"When you identify only with your ego and all of its assumptions and judgments, you are making your opinions the be all and end all, when they actually have little to do with anything or anyone except you. By identifying with them completely, you are diminishing your identity and making your 'reality' all about you and these judgments."

"I'm not about to give up my concept of who I am. I have to judge for myself so that my life turns out the way I want," Bud said.

"When you shift your awareness and embrace the Great Love, Bud, you're still everything you thought you were—and you can be that at any time—only now you are so much more!"

Bud thought about what the Master was saying. He was able to see the ego-self he had created as something he possessed, not all that he was. "I'm starting to grasp what you're saying. If I did decide to open up like that, what would I actually have to do?"

"Bud, there are two steps to the process of shifting your consciousness from ego to the Great Love. First, you hold yourself entirely accountable for your perceptions."

"I am choosing to see the world the way I do, and I can at any time choose to see it another way. Right?"

"Exactly!" said the Master, "You can and we all can."

"What is the second step you mentioned?"

"The second step is very similar; it brings the first step to the next level," the Master continued. "You acknowledge the power of your intention. If you want to do something and it materializes, it is because your intention was powerful enough to become solidified."

"I don't know if I completely understand that, Master," Bud said with a frown.

"When you want to have an experience, you project the thought of it onto the screen of your personal reality and then you step into that scene and it becomes real."

Bud sat in contemplation of the Master's words. "That still sounds to me like I'm just doing my own thing. It doesn't sound like the Great Love you described."

"The principal works the same way, whether you define yourself as an ego or as all that is. When we create our reality from our petty little ego, we create a petty little world. If we were to shift our identity from the ego to the Great Love, together we could create a magnificent world."

"I don't want to unite with others," Bud said fervently. "I don't want to be a part of one consciousness. I want to be myself and have my own mind."

"You already are part of one consciousness, Bud. It is the consciousness of the earth we live on. The earth is the solidification of a collective state of mind, and anyone who dwells upon it is a cell in the body of the planet."

"Are you saying that I need to relinquish my ego identity and merge with the consciousness of the planet?"

"Yes. Now here comes the part I think you will like."

"Well, that's good," said Bud, "because I don't like what you just told me."

"While it may seem as if you are giving up your independent self in exchange for being part of the Great Love, you actually become more authentically who you are."

"How can that be?"

"You are not your ego, Bud. You were part of the Great Love when you started building your ego, and you are part of the Great Love right now. That is your authentic self, and that is who you will always be."

"Well then why create an ego in the first place?"

"Every time you spoke your truth and someone shot you down for it you started building a wall around yourself. Every time you felt negated or overpowered you put another brick on that wall. You weren't really overpowered; you just felt that you were. You are the one who diminished your power. You gave more credibility to the other person than you did to your own truth. You reacted to anything you didn't like, anything that didn't feel good, by burying the love in your heart and moving into fear and defensiveness. If you had responded with love, you would have saved yourself some heartache and you might have disarmed the people you thought were trying to hurt you."

After that last remark, Bud became pensive. He moved into a deeper space, and then he changed the subject. "Tell me Master, what am I doing here? What is my reason for being?"

"No one can answer that for another person. It is up to you to answer that question with your life. Let's review. We looked at how you are responsible for your experience of reality and that you have the power to manifest your intention. You're starting to see that your true self is something greater than your ego. So

I don't think your answer to the question is going to be about getting your own way. I suspect it will have something to do with contributing to a world that is more full of love. Don't you think?"

"With all the fear and hatred in the world, that sure sounds like a tall order!"

"You can do it though, my young friend, if you are willing and able to open up your heart. Then you will realize that success in life has little to do with material accomplishment because your life here on earth is transitory."

"Then what does constitute success?" Bud asked.

"When you cease arguing with life. When you withstand the tough times without taking it personally. When you remain centered in your heart. When you demonstrate faith that what you are going through is the perfect lesson for the time. Never forget, Bud, that you are a valued part of humanity and that everything happens for a reason that will ultimately benefit all of us."

"Thank you, Master Wiseheart. You've allowed me to step out of myself and see a bigger picture. You are such a source of inspiration and I am so happy that I met you."

"Before you go, let me give a powerful phrase that will help cement the new way of thinking into your consciousness. Say this affirmation aloud, if you can, several times a day. If you catch yourself reverting to your ego-based thinking, say 'Cancel that thought!' and repeat this phrase. Do this for twenty-one days and you will see a permanent change in your outlook and behavior. Are you willing to do that?"

"Yes, I am. What is the phrase?"

"Why not write it down, Bud, as I give it to you?"

> **I now choose to honor
> my authentic self and express
> the Great Love that I am.**

The Master's words reverberated in his mind as he wrote them down.

As Bud drove back to his house he realized his life was going to change. Instead of allowing egotism to motivate him, he was going to act from his authentic self. Sure, he was still going to do as he pleased. Only now, as a result of his meeting with Master Wiseheart, his sense of identity was enlarging. The person he thought he was, the separate and independent self, was growing and attaining a universal identity, an identity that felt connected to all that is.

Bud made up his mind that from that point on he was going to honor everything that came to him and to see it as a gift. Never again would he hurt or compete with others. He had grounded himself in the Great Love and his world was on its way to becoming a lighter and freer place.

LESSON TWO

MOLLY – "I need more stuff"

Bud had never been interested in Molly as a girlfriend. She was short, kind of stocky, and rarely had anything new or exciting to say. Still, when he ran into her on a shopping spree, where she seemed to have bought out the store, he was happy to help carry her packages to her car.

"What on earth is in all these bags, Molly?"

"Oh, I bought lots of new clothes," Molly began, "some shoes I couldn't resist, a new comforter for my bed, some towels that were on sale, and a book on a diet I haven't tried yet. Oh, maybe I shouldn't have told you that last part."

Bud had a soft spot in his heart for Molly. She was natural and down to earth. She never acted as if she was impressed with herself—just with her stuff. Bud saw nothing wrong with Molly's appreciation of beautiful things, but she was so focused on what she could acquire. 'If only she could realize that life was about giving,' thought Bud as he walked her to her car. 'I wonder if I could get her to go see the Master.'

"So, I haven't seen you in a while," Molly said, "What's new with you?"

"Nothing much," Bud said. "Well, except that I had this amazing encounter with a man I guess you'd have to call a sage, or a mystic. He really opened my eyes to the truth."

"Really?" Molly exclaimed, surprised that Bud would listen to anyone. "What did he have to say?"

"Actually I think what he says is so specific to each person that you would really have to speak with him yourself."

"There is something that I would like some advice on. If this man is as wise as you seem to think, he may be just the person who could help me. Do we have to call first?"

"No, you don't even have to knock on the door, you just go right in. I'd be glad to take you there. Let's go right now."

"How much does he charge?" Molly inquired.

"He doesn't charge. It's free," answered Bud.

"Then how can it be worth anything?" said Molly with a confused look on her face.

"Haven't you ever heard that the best things in life are free, Molly?"

"They're not," Molly said vehemently. "Everything costs something and the best things cost the most."

"You're talking about physical objects, things we pay money for because they're useful in our lives," said Bud. "I'm talking about experiences that are beyond price, such as the experience of love."

"There are some things that are priceless, I'll grant you that. We all need more, though, to stay alive. This wise man you speak of, I mean, doesn't he need to make a living?"

"I suspect he lives such a simple life that he hardly needs any money."

"He must be very deprived," said Molly.

"He didn't seem that way to me," Bud replied. "Master Wiseheart, that's his name by the way, appears to be very much at peace. That is what impressed me about him. He is so comfortable and content with who he is that sitting in his presence is a calming experience. I can't quite explain it. You know, it's sort of a Zen experience—do you know about the philosophy of Zen?"

"Not really," said Molly.

"It's about accepting the world exactly as it is."

"All right, let's go and see him. What have I got to lose?"

"Only your pain," said Bud.

From Greed to Gratitude

"I have brought my friend Molly to see you today, Master Wiseheart," said Bud as he and Molly entered the tent. The wise man was again in the center of the round room sitting in the lotus position. He had on the same style robe, only this time the color of his robe was brown instead of red.

"What would you like to discuss, Molly?" inquired the Master.

After hesitating for a moment, Molly responded to the Master's question. "I have put so much energy into acquiring the best things money can buy. Lately, though, I'm noticing that things don't really fill up the emptiness I feel inside. I'm beginning to realize that my material belongings will never love me back."

"No, they never will," said the Master speaking in a compassionate tone.

"Still, I hate to give anything up," Molly continued. "I keep thinking I need more and more stuff. I'm afraid that one day I'll lose what I have."

"This issue is very common," said the Master.

"What can I do about it?"

"Two things, Molly. First of all, be grateful for what you have. When you stay in a space of gratitude, you generate a powerful energy that attracts never-ending abundance into your life. It is the reflection of your value coming back to you."

"Sometimes I feel that I don't have any value," Molly said.

"As you are beginning to see, your value has nothing to do with what you have managed to acquire. It comes from knowing who you are and sharing that with the world. And that brings us to the second thing you can do: Realize that material stability comes through giving."

"Giving!" Molly recoiled. "Isn't that the opposite of acquiring? Won't I have less?"

"Molly, when you focus on what you don't have and attempt to correct that by acquiring more, you diminish yourself. Your emptiness grows. On the other hand, when you focus on what you have to give, you make yourself larger. Your fullness expands."

"Having the things I like around me makes me feel good," declared Molly.

"When you think that material objects are a source of joy in your life," the Master continued, "it is a regression back to a time of idol worship. It is the quality of your life that is important, not the quantity."

"Well how would you define quality of life?"

"A person can be happy with very few possessions or miserable with many. Things in themselves do not provide happiness. It is how you feel about yourself that matters."

"I could not be happy living as you do, Master," said Molly. "Owning things makes me feel that I have more worth in the world."

The Master remained perfectly calm as he continued the dialogue. "The time has come to shift the concept of value from a purely monetary identification to a more humane one. When you discover your innate worth you can be happy no matter what happens."

"What about the freedom that wealth provides?" Molly asked the Master.

"If you emphasize material values over values that are more nourishing to the soul, such as loving relationships, then your life becomes more subject to pressure and control. You are less free and thus less happy. The emptiness you describe becomes more and more painful."

Molly seemed somewhat dejected as she considered the Master's words. She looked to Bud for moral support. He just grinned with an 'isn't this guy great?' look. She felt that what the Master was saying had to be the truth; she just wasn't comfortable with it.

"Hmmm...I can sense that you're right," Molly said to the Master. "I just don't see how to change my life. If I let go of my current value system, I don't feel I have anything to replace it with. I have tried sitting as you do in a meditative trance and quite frankly, wise man, that doesn't do it for me the way a new car or a beautiful new wardrobe or jewelry would. It doesn't give me something that makes my life more comfortable, such as a plush armchair or a new mattress for my bed. It's not something I can sink my teeth into like a filet mignon or a crème brulée."

"The material world is ours to enjoy," said the Master. "Still, we are stewards of this beautiful planet. It is essential that all of us who live on the earth immediately begin thinking in terms of sustaining life for future generations. This can be accomplished by practicing a more moderate lifestyle, conserving more and consuming less."

"If I become less acquisitive, Master, will I truly be happier? Will I have what I need?"

"You don't need anything, Molly. The reason people are greedy in the outer world is because they feel empty in their inner world. They are not empty though; they are closed, because they allowed the world to hurt them, or they expected that it would."

"How can I make sure that does not happen in my life any more?"

"The new currency is love, Molly, and heart connections are the new means of exchange. The love you experience is the truest measure of your worth in the world. The intrinsic value of love cannot be diminished nor can love's essence ever be destroyed. As your mind is filled with light and your heart is filled with love the power to manifest whatever contributes to your purpose is yours for life."

"A part of me wants to believe what you say," Molly said.

"Then listen to that part of you," replied the Master. "And to help you with that, I will leave you with a powerful phrase that you can use to remind yourself of this new way of looking at things. Say this aloud several times a day, and whenever you find yourself feeling needy in some way. Here is your affirmation. Please write this down."

> **Whatever supports my purpose is available to me, and I am grateful for all that I have to share.**

Tears welled up in Molly's eyes. "Thank you, Master Wiseheart," she said, "and thank you, Bud, for bringing me here."

LESSON THREE

STEVEN – "I need to know more"

Bud and Molly ran into their friend Steven at the library. Steven was the smartest kid in their class. He even looked intelligent in his horn-rimmed glasses and preppy attire.

Steven came across with a know-it-all attitude, yet secretly his fear was that he didn't know enough.

"I want to have an answer to everything," Steven confessed to his friends, "but I'm hardly making a dent in any subject I study. Everyone has a different opinion and the facts keep changing all the time. It's as if I live in a maze of inconsistencies. It seems to me that all truth is relative and that there are no easy explanations. What can anyone be sure of?"

"Perhaps no one is sure of anything," Bud replied.

"That is a very unsettling thought, Bud," said Molly. "Maybe that's why I try to hold on to things, although that is starting to change."

"To me it's not about accumulating stuff, it's about gathering ideas," Steven said. "I think ideas are the most important things in the world. The problem is, they often contradict each other and it's downright confusing."

"I like looking at life in different ways," said Bud. "We have two sides to our brain after all. What we see and hear is based on which side of the brain we are using. There's the left side that processes facts and figures. Then there's the right side, the creative half of the team."

"So let's see," said Steven, trying to be funny, "if I use two heads, I'll always be right."

"No one is always right, Steven," said Bud.

"If I could just tell what's really important, I could delve more deeply into what matters. To me, everything's interesting but nothing's all that important."

"Something becomes important because you care about it, Steven," Molly said. "Don't you care about anything?"

"I care about lots of things, but not for very long. Actually, the main thing I care about is not being stuck in any absolute way of thinking. That would be boring."

"It sounds to me as if you're just skimming the surface of life," Molly said. "You're just licking the icing on the cake without getting to the good stuff inside."

"And there you've just said what my problem is," Steven said.

"You know, Steven," said Molly, "why don't we go over and see Master Wiseheart? He's the one who really knows what matters. Bud took me to see him and both of us are just amazed at what we learned."

"Yeah, he sure helped me," Bud said.

"How did he help you?" Steven asked.

"He told me to get out of my own way. He reminded me that there is this enormous energy, the Great Love, which is available to everyone. Once you embrace this energy, you always know what's important. It's as if you're being guided by higher forces."

"That sounds kind of far out," Steven said, "but I wouldn't mind checking out what this man has to say. I'll make up my own mind of course."

"I'll write down the directions on how to get there," said Bud. "If I were you, I'd go right away."

From Superficiality to Awareness

When took Steven entered the tent, the Master was in the center of the yurt in the lotus position, in a long orange robe.

"Hello, Master Wiseheart. I'm Steven. I'm a friend of Bud and Molly."

"Greetings, Steven. What is on your mind?" inquired the Master.

"What's on my mind? Well, that's just it! Everything's on my mind, but nothing means anything. My friends are suggesting that I go more deeply into things, but I can't seem to decide what's important and what's not. Besides that, there is so much information to cover, I can barely scratch the surface of any one subject. I want to avoid a situation where I don't have enough information to know what to do."

"The information you want is available to you," the Master said as Steven listened intently. "Simply make sure there is room in your brain to absorb it."

"How do I clear some space in my mind?" asked Steven. "Ideas keep flowing through my consciousness like quicksilver. I can entertain the possibility of just about anything."

"You are giving your attention to nonessentials because you're afraid you're going to miss something. By doing that, what you're missing is the point! You end up with superficial knowledge and you never get to the heart of the matter."

"I know," Steven admitted. "I'm a jack of all trades and a master of none. I know a little bit about almost everything but not enough about anything."

"Steven," the Master said, "if you give your undivided attention to the present moment, it will reveal to you deeper layers of information."

"How can I make sure that I get the right answers?" inquired Steven.

"The answers you get are based on the questions you ask. If you want different answers, ask different questions."

"I've been asking questions all my life. When I was a kid, nobody ever wanted to explore my questions. They couldn't get past the conventional answers and come up with some new ways of looking at things. They just wanted to stay locked into their comfort zone where everything was always the same and never changed."

"The answers don't come from other people, Steven. The answers come as you listen to what other people and the world have to say and you hear it in your own way. Your inner voice will give you the information that is reflective of your current situation rather than someone else's story."

"Sometimes I can't hear my own voice because I've got so many people in my face telling me where it's at."

"You need to listen to what your own inner knowing is telling you, Steven, rather than looking outside you for answers. The things that show up around you can be perceived as messages to guide you with some skilled interpretation on your part."

"How can it be up to me to interpret the world? I'm interested in the facts, not some story I make up."

"You're making it all up, Steven. Life has a flow. That flow is the Great Love and it is responsive to your suggestion."

"I've heard about the Great Love and I still don't know what it is."

"The Great Love is the universe in love with itself, creating itself and realizing itself through you, Steven. Nothing that shows up in your space is there accidentally. It is there because you put it there."

"I did? I put it there?"

"Well, of course. Don't be so modest. What you see around you is the outgrowth of all your thoughts and fears, your hopes and your dreams. The more you put your mental energy into manifesting an idea, the more solid it becomes."

"So no matter where I go," said Steven, "what happens is I keep connecting with the products of my own mind?"

"Yes," said the Master, "and whenever you want to, you can change what shows up in your space by changing the content of your thoughts. Essentially the world is fluid, not solid. When you concentrate on new ideas, then they are the ones that will solidify and replace the older ideas."

"Well, I need to know more about how to do that," Steven said.

Master Wiseheart corrected Steven immediately. "You said 'need.' Thinking that you need anything only serves to create anxiety, and that casts a shadow on the pure awareness that you are. It is the petty part of us that needs. The magnificent part of us already is whole and complete."

Steven mulled over the Master's words. "I'll need to—oops!—I'll think about what you've told me," he said.

"There's no need to think, Steven. You *are* awareness. Just relax into it. Then the information you are looking for will be presented to you when it's important to know it."

"Thank you, Master Wiseheart."

"Before you go, let me leave you with a powerful phrase, an affirmation, that will help remind you of what we talked about today. Whenever you feel scattered, say it aloud. Please write this down and refer to it often."

> **As I give my undivided attention
> to the present moment,
> the information I seek is revealed to me.**

"I'm going to take your advice," Steven said as he stood up to leave, "and I'm going to mention you to a few of my friends."

LESSON FOUR

MARJORIE – "I need to protect myself"

As it turned out, the very next day, Steven was invited to a small dinner party at his friend Marjorie's house. Marjorie was one of the prettiest and nicest girls he knew, a blonde-haired, blue-eyed sweetheart whom he often thought of as riding an emotional roller coaster most of the time.

Steven didn't quite understand emotions very well. He would have them on occasion, yet he was usually successful in ignoring them. Instead, he experienced an emotional life vicariously through friends like Marjorie. Steven appreciated his friendship with her, even though the two of them were very different.

At the party, all Steven could talk about was his experience with Master Wiseheart.

"Do you think the Master could help me resolve an issue I have that worries me?" Marjorie asked, suddenly looking like she was going to cry.

"Marjorie, you don't seem to have anything to worry about. Your folks are the richest people in town."

"That's what concerns me," Marjorie replied. "Look at how we live."

"I am looking," said Steven. "Why, this place is a mansion!"

"I think of it more as a prison," said Marjorie. "When you arrive here, the first thing that greets you is a big, heavy wrought iron gate and six dogs with blood curdling barks yowling at you. My parents are afraid that people want to take things away from them. They even keep a gun on hand just in case someone tries."

"You know," said Steven, "what I learned from Master Wiseheart is that our life is the result of what we think. For instance, if you think people are going to take something from you, you're giving power to that possibility. You're increasing the chances that in some way it will happen."

Marjorie took in what Steven was saying and sat with it for a moment. "I think I have inherited my parent's fears," she admitted. "I don't feel this world we live in is a safe place. Not now, at least, and maybe not ever. I would like to meet the wise man and hear what he has to say to me," she said. "Maybe he can help me find some peace of mind."

From Insecurity to Trust

As the dinner party drew to a close and the other guests left, Steven and Marjorie made their way over to Master Wiseheart's tent.

'At least,' thought Steven, 'Marjorie will get to bask in the radiant presence of the Master. Maybe he'll explain why so many people on earth feel insecure, since that seems to be Marjorie's main issue.'

"Just go on in, Marjorie. I'll wait for you here in the car," said Steven.

Marjorie walked inside the round tent, and there in the center was a man seated in the lotus position, wearing a shimmering silver robe. There were lighted candles everywhere and incense was burning.

Marjorie timidly addressed the Master. "May I speak with you?"

"Of course, Marjorie. Don't be shy," the Master replied warmly.

"You called me Marjorie."

"That is your name."

"Yes, it is, but how did you know that? We've never met before."

A mysterious grin appeared on the master's face. "Is there something troubling you?"

"There is," Marjorie replied. "I might as well come right out with it. I don't feel safe living in this world."

"You're living in your own world, Marjorie. Why are you creating it to be unsafe?" asked the Master.

"Master, it was created long before I ever arrived."

"What was, Marjorie?"

"The world."

"I'm not talking about *the* world, Marjorie. I'm talking about your own personal world—the world that belongs to you and you alone. Wherever you go, the psychic space you inhabit is your own creation. This is probably more obvious to you in the quiet moments when you are alone, when the vivid inner life you experience is a reality that only you know. The same principle is at work, however, when there is a lot of stimulation. At all times, regardless of the outside circumstances, you are living in your inner world. That is your true home, and you can create it as a sacred space."

"I know what you mean about my inner world," said Marjorie, "but even if I create the sacred space you describe, there's still so much negativity to deal with in this life."

"Can you state an example?" asked the Master. "Just one if you will, Marjorie, so as to give me an idea of what you mean by negativity."

Marjorie's emotions, previously guarded up to now, burst out. "Isn't it obvious, Master Wiseheart? Just look at all those terrible stories in the newspaper. People getting robbed or hurt in some way. Wars! Natural disasters! Starvation! There are so many victims in this world and I am afraid of becoming one of them."

"You're a very sensitive person, Marjorie," the Master said. "You need a lot of quiet time where you can go deep inside yourself and create a secret garden, a sanctuary for your soul, a place where you feel your spirit is connected to the universe. That is the true source of your security. Instead of contracting when you confront a worrisome situation, what you want to do is expand your sense of connection and see it from a larger perspective. This will enable you to trust that you can overcome fear with love."

"But what if harm comes to me?"

"Marjorie, you are not a helpless person living in a hostile universe—unless you believe that you are. When you are afraid of being vulnerable, the world will reflect your inner fears back to you. When, instead, you are open and trusting, your loving approach to any situation will keep you out of harm's way."

"Are you telling me" asked Marjorie, "that my fears actually attract danger? So to a great extent, I am responsible for my own personal safety. Is that true?"

"You are responsible for everything that you bring into your life. If you worry about being safe it will not actually make you safer; instead you will paint yourself into a corner and limit your potential to grow. Then you will be stuck in a narrow world indeed."

"You are so right!" said Marjorie. "My family lives in a big house with lots of land around it, but the world in their minds is so restrictive."

"Like most of us, your family wants to have a life of greater ease and comfort. Still, our fear that something on the outside could harm us compels us to build a wall of false security, a wall that actually blocks the flow of positive energies that could bring something better into our lives."

Marjorie wanted to learn more. "How can I tear down the wall and grow into a space of trust?"

"Marjorie, there are two different ways of perceiving life. One is through your mind. A lot of people, for better or worse, contributed to all that is in your mind—parents, teachers, friends, the media. Everyone you have ever spoken with and everything you have ever read has filled your mind with someone else's story."

"That's the reality I'm most familiar with, Master. You said there was another way of perceiving life."

"The other way is through your heart. No one else painted a picture for you of the world that lives in your heart."

"How is that way different?" asked Marjorie.

"Your heart has no boundaries. It is your universal self, the part of you that is unlimited. Once you are connected with your universal self, no matter how bleak your situation, you will realize that conditions will not always be that way."

"How do I connect with my universal self?" Marjorie asked.

"If you were not already connected," he replied, "you would not have come here today."

"How can I connect more deeply? I would like to be as connected as you are."

"First," said the Master, "you have to want the connection to become deeper, as you apparently do. Secondly, you have to believe that it's possible. When you believe it, you will see it. Close your eyes and let's do a process."

Marjorie gladly complied.

"Now," said the Master, "imagine that you are in a space of absolute safety and serenity. Bring your consciousness into the light and feel the love that emanates from your innermost being." The Master paused in silence to allow Marjorie some time. "Stay there in that space."

"For how long?" asked Marjorie.

"Forever," replied the Master.

A very long silence ensued. As she sat with Master Wiseheart in this marvelous meditative space they shared Marjorie felt that something wonderful and healing was taking place.

"When you are ready," the Master said softly, "gently open your eyes and come back into the room."

"I am beginning to feel that what is inside me is so much greater than anything that comes from the outside," she said.

"The more you dwell in the presence of your inner light, the more secure you will feel," said the Master. "Your consciousness is now deeply rooted in your true nature. You have made a heart connection with yourself."

"Is this what Steven referred to as the Great Love?"

"Yes it is, Marjorie. How do you feel now?"

"I feel like everything is going to be all right. There's really nothing to worry about because I can always return to that special place that we just went to in the meditation."

"You never really leave that special place, Marjorie, unless you choose to believe something other than the truth. This is a benevolent universe. It sends you the energy that is most supportive of your intentions. If you reject this energy because you don't like the package it comes in, you will continue looking for something that will prove to be less effective."

Marjorie sat there for a while and felt a deep sense of appreciation for what had just occurred. Then she got an idea.

"Master Wiseheart, I have a friend named Max. I feel he could benefit from the advice you give. Perhaps you can offer him some inspiration."

"Tell your friend to visit whenever he wants."

"I will," said Marjorie.

"Marjorie, before you go, let me give you an affirmation you can say aloud throughout the day, particularly when you feel afraid of anything. Please write this down."

> **I am safe and secure
> because I am connected to my source
> and have faith in the goodness of life.**

"That's what I learned here today, Master. Thank you."

"Goodbye, Marjorie, and remember, when you perceive life with your heart, you realize that your outer reality is the result of your inner state of being."

LESSON FIVE

MAX – "I need to be somebody"

Steven and Marjorie were having lunch on the campus lawn when they saw their friend Max off in the distance.

"Max thinks he's God's gift to the world," Marjorie said. "Although I do have to admit, he is an Adonis."

"He is kind of full of himself isn't he?" asked Steven.

"Perhaps Max doesn't have enough love in his life and he tries to compensate."

"Do any of us have enough love?" asked Steven

"No," said Marjorie. "I guess not. I think I can persuade Max to talk to Master Wiseheart," said Marjorie. "Let me try him on his cell phone."

Max answered and Marjorie said, "Max, Steven and I saw you walking across campus. We wondered if you had been to see that wise man who's living in the woods."

"Oh, the Master. Yeah, Bud told me about him. I was thinking about going."

"We're in front of the library," Marjorie said as she waved to Max. "Why don't you come on over here and we'll fill you in on our experiences with him."

"Oh, I see you! OK, I'll be right there."

From Pride to Generosity

Something powerful must have struck Max during his conversation with Marjorie and Steven. He left right away to see the Master.

"Master Wiseheart," said Max upon entering the round tent. "I have heard about you from my friends. They are very impressed with your counsel. I don't usually do this sort of thing."

"What sort of thing?" the Master responded.

"I don't usually seek advice. I take my own."

"That's a good idea," said the wise man.

Max was surprised at this remark. "It is?"

Just then Max noticed how intense the Master's eyes were. The Master radiated a powerful energy accentuated by his resplendent yellow robe.

"Sit down, my young friend. How can I be of assistance?" asked the Master.

Max took a few moments to respond. "Well, you see, all my life I have wanted to impress the world with how special I am. I was happy when others praised me, and that gave me confidence. When they criticized me, it was as if something in me shut down."

"Why did people criticize you?"

"They said I always insisted on being the main attraction. I have to admit, I do love attention. It's as if I am always hungry, but it's not food I'm hungry for, it's love."

Master Wiseheart listened to Max's disclosure. "Your apprehension about being unloved stems from a false belief, Max. You picked up this belief in the school of fear."

"The school of fear? What's that?"

"It's a story the whole world has bought into, in which you're taught to believe that you're separate from everyone around you. It all started with Adam and Eve. They wanted to be individuals and be in charge of their destiny so they left paradise and began making their own choices. Once they were disconnected from their source, they realized that their powers had diminished. The contrast between the abundance they had before in a state of unity and the weakness they now felt as separate beings gave rise to fear and a false need to be important. They believed they needed to be somebody, when in fact they already were."

"If Adam and Eve were originally perfect, why did they make this mistake?"

"It was not a mistake. It was the only way they could experience at the deepest level the power of choice. Once they believed the state of separation their minds had created, they felt a need to inflate their self-importance. It was a vain attempt to demonstrate that their ego-created self was superior to their natural, universal self. They had to work a lot harder because they were no longer tapping in to the unlimited creative energy that was the source of their being. They had made themselves so small by identifying primarily with their ego that they lost sight of their original greatness."

"Why do you call it the school of fear?"

"The fear that comes from separation motivates people to act in ways that bring about their greatest lessons. Perhaps the ultimate lesson is that when you stop pretending to be somebody and start expressing who you really are, there is no longer anything to fear. Then all conflicts come to a close and the desire to separate from the whole is gone forever."

Then the Master closed his eyes and as he did this, Max noticed that the wise man's aura seemed to be expanding. 'Is this what Marjorie was referring to when she spoke of the Great Love?' Max wondered. Then a smile came upon the Master's face. 'Yes,' Max thought, 'surely the Master is imbued with a love that is beyond this world, a love so great that just being in the presence of it makes me feel better.'

Max continued baring his soul. "People keep telling me I have a lot of pride, and I do," he admitted. "There is nothing wrong with that, is there? I want to like and feel good about myself, and that part is fine I think. What happens, though, is that people keep telling me I'm a show-off. You see, Master, I believe in my talents and I think I have a great future."

"Your future," said the Master, "will be determined less by your talents and more by how much you want it and how much the world wants you to have it."

"I do want it, but in order to rise to the occasion, I have to feel that I'm loved. If love fails me, I don't know if I can make it."

"Love will never fail you, but you might fail love if you try to stand out and be better than others. You are attempting to get your ego self to become as big as the Great Love that you really are."

"Marjorie mentioned this to me. What exactly do you mean by the Great Love?" Max asked his mentor.

"The Great Love is love without reservation and it is available to everyone who wishes to channel it. It is a radiation of self-love that becomes universal as soon as it is shared. It is not directed to anyone in particular. Once you are touched by it, your relationship with life is enhanced. You become a vessel for an immense energy that is the heart and soul of every living thing, an energy whose scope knows no bounds. When that expression comes into full bloom, you become a conduit for a force that can be used to elevate the world."

"That sounds like the highest a person could aspire to," said Max. "I'm not sure I'm ready for that, but if I did want to move in that direction, what would I need to do?"

"Simply witness and honor the dance of life, and participate in it without seeking to being praised or adored in return. Rather than attempting to ascend in a blaze of glory, replace vanity and boastfulness with a quiet dignity."

"That is so beautiful," said Max. "I wonder if I could really be like that."

"Max, you are blessed by what you have to give. As you embrace the Great Love you will feel that you are overflowing with radiant light, and all you will want to do is share it with each person you meet. Open your heart until love generously pours out from you."

"It's just a slight shift in how I look at things isn't it, Master? I mean I always have felt that I had a lot to give," said Max. "What I was afraid of was that it would not come back to me."

"Once you allow the universe to shine its light and love through you, you become part of a co-creative process. Then what you have yearned for, what you have been trying to achieve every day of your life, becomes an effortless part of your life. People do notice you. People do admire your efforts. The irony of it all is that now what matters to you is giving what you have, rather than needing to take the credit and take the bows."

"In a way it's funny, Master Wiseheart," said Max. "I thought it was so important to be somebody, but the somebody I wanted to be doesn't hold a candle to what you have told me I can be — a part of the Great Love. Thank you Master, I am glad I came to see you today."

"So am I, Max. Before you go, let me leave you with an affirmation that will remind you of what we talked about today. If you catch yourself looking for attention or recognition, just repeat this phrase and you'll get yourself headed in the right direction again. Please write this down."

> **I get out of my own way
> so that the Great Love that I am
> comes through me to be shared with everyone.**

"Master Wiseheart, you're a genius!" said Max as he left the tent grinning from ear to ear.

LESSON SIX

Agnes – "I need to be helpful"

Max rushed back to the school to share with his friends what he had just experienced in the presence of the Master. He didn't see Steven or Marjorie anywhere. In fact the entire campus was practically deserted. Just as he was about to leave, he saw someone he recognized quietly sitting under a tree reading a book. It was Agnes.

Max knew that Agnes liked him, yet he had never paid much attention to her. Now, as he stood there watching her, he realized why. Max liked girls who were flashy and glamorous and Agnes was as far from that as anyone he knew. Why then, he wondered, did he now feel as if he wanted to go over and strike up a conversation with her?

From the corner of her eye, Agnes could see Max standing there watching her. 'That's funny,' she thought. 'Why, all of a sudden, is he interested in me?'

"Hi, Agnes," said Max. "What are you doing here?"

"Well," she answered, "I really didn't feel like going home."

"How come?"

"I'm not very happy at home," she confessed.

"Why is that?" asked Max. "Do they mistreat you?"

"Oh no, nothing like that. They ignore me, the way most people do."

"I'm sorry to hear that," Max said, feeling a tinge of guilt.

For a while, neither Max nor Agnes said a word. Max broke the silence. "Today has been such an incredible day for me."

"Why? What happened?"

"What happened? Nothing short of a miracle came into my life!" declared Max.

Agnes scowled. "I'm too skeptical to believe in miracles."

"I don't think you'd be a skeptic if you met this wise man I just went to visit."

"Wise man?" Agnes asked.

Max grinned. "That's right. His name is Master Wiseheart."

"What pearls of wisdom did you glean from him?"

"He told me that we're all part of the Great Love and that we've been enrolled in the school of fear."

"Now that last part I can believe."

"Agnes, you are cynical indeed. The school of fear has a purpose."

"And what is its purpose, pray tell? Why do we have fear in the first place?" Agnes asked. "Why can't there just be love?"

"For the same reason we have day and night. If there were no darkness, we would have no appreciation of what light is. That is why Adam and Eve left the Garden of Eden."

"I always wondered about that one," Agnes said, rolling her eyes. "Why did they leave?"

"They shifted their consciousness and everything split in two."

"What?" Agnes said, reacting in disbelief.

"Adam and Eve wanted to have a deeper experience of the world and duality was the way to have it."

"You know, Max, I think a miracle did happen for you today!"

"Thanks." Max was glad to hear Agnes acknowledge that something wonderful had occurred in his life. "I guess you're not as much of a skeptic as you say you are."

"Oh yes, I am. I deal in concrete realities. I believe what I see."

"It could also be said that you see what you believe." Max countered. "That is what Master Wiseheart told my friend Marjorie. First, you have to want something. Then you have to believe it is possible. Then it can happen. When you believe it enough, in time you will see it."

"That's all there is to it, Max? You make it sound utterly magical."

"Well no. There is work involved. The more we take our beliefs seriously and put energy into manifesting them, the more substantial our return will be."

"Now you're beginning to make sense. I don't expect to get results without effort. Besides, I like to be busy. It calms my nerves."

"I've always noticed that you work hard and I know you get very good grades," Max said.

"Some people have accused me of being a perfectionist. Do you think that is a bad thing to be, Max?"

"No, Agnes, of course not. Unless you take it too far."

"I just cannot bear disorder," Agnes admitted. "I'm always noticing what's not right and it makes me critical of everything."

"Well, I think that when you focus on the imperfections of everything around you, it diverts your attention from your own flaws."

"Ouch," said Agnes. "I suppose that could be true."

"Agnes, let me take you over to see Master Wiseheart. You can talk about this issue with him and I think he'll be able to shed a great deal of light on your situation."

From Criticism to Humility

Max and Agnes entered the yurt and found Master Wiseheart meditating. This time the color of the robe he was wearing was beige.

The Master opened his eyes suddenly and his face lit up as he looked at his visitors. "How lovely," the Master said. "Look what destiny has brought to me today!"

Max beamed.

Agnes frowned.

"Master Wiseheart," said Max, "this is Agnes."

As the Master looked at Agnes, his penetrating gaze made her feel a bit self-conscious. "Tell me, Agnes, what would you like to discuss?"

"Can you help me? I'm never happy with the way things are. I'm just too critical."

"Why are you that way?" asked Master Wiseheart.

"When I see something is wrong I want to fix it. It's because I want to be helpful, but I'm not having much fun. I'm always getting stuck with the details that nobody else wants to deal with."

"Why does everything have to be so perfect?" Max asked Agnes.

"I don't know," Agnes replied.

"There are as many versions of perfection as there are people," the Master said. "Why do you feel that you are the only one who can see what needs to be done?"

"Nobody seems to care as much as I do about doing things the right way."

"Did it ever occur to you, Agnes, that you have a fear of inadequacy? Perhaps this is what drives you to be busy all the time and makes you critical as well."

"Well, I'm the only one who knows how to do everything correctly. Why would I be afraid of being inadequate?"

"It's because you want to be perfect, but the only way to be perfect is to be loving. If you are not coming from love, you are doing everyone a disservice, yourself included. Work done in the pursuit of perfection is conceit. Your true calling is to be in the service of love."

"I never thought of myself as being conceited," said Agnes, stunned by what the wise man was telling her.

"If you think you are the only one who knows how to do the job correctly," replied the Master, "is that not conceit?"

"Well, yes, I suppose it is. I never looked at it that way." Agnes did not want to hear this but she could not turn away from the truth that was being given to her.

'I guess by focusing on the one thing that is wrong,' she thought to herself, 'I have been ignoring all the things that are right. It's almost a curse to focus on the flaws all the time.'

Then, as if a ray of hope was coming over her, Agnes asked, "What can I do to change the way I see things so that my experiences become more positive?"

"Relax into an awareness of the Great Love, which is who you really are. Make an effort to abandon your slavish adherence to impossibly high standards. Even if your methods are efficient, they are not addressing the most important issue in your life and that is how to be more loving."

"Will life become easier for me if I do that?"

"As you open up your heart," said the Master, "the light that emanates from you transforms drudgery into a labor of love. Once you cease worrying over trifles, you actually will enhance your proficiency. It is not helpful to analyze your circumstances to death. When instead you allow the available energies to flow through you effortlessly, you will become a vessel for enlightened service."

"I'm a pragmatist, Master," said Agnes. "What is the value of what you are saying? What will the net result be?"

"Humility. It is one of the most precious attributes a human being can have. Humility is a virtue that will enable you to depersonalize your experience and connect with a higher and a more powerful energy. It is the key to accessing the Great Love, yet it is given only to those without any desire for power over others. Humility and the Great Love are always present together. Unless one has humility, other people are seen either as a means to enhance one's ego or as a threat that could tear it down."

"I never heard anyone describe humility that way. Most people think it's not desirable to be humble. You seem to be saying that humility is a way for me to be at peace with the way things are. That's a big change for me. I think it's going to take some time to put this into practice. I don't even know if I can."

"I want to give you an affirmation that will help you, Agnes. Repeat this throughout the day, and especially whenever you find yourself resorting to criticism. Please write this down."

> **I focus on the positive
> and make things better by offering
> my loving attention as a service.**

"Thank you for your teaching, Master. This has been very helpful. You have given me some excellent guidelines and I intend to follow them."

"Blessings," said the Master, bowing his head slightly and cupping his hands.

Agnes and Max returned the gesture.

BRETT – "I need to be with someone"

Most of the students who heard about the encounters with Master Wiseheart responded as if they were listening to a fairy tale. It was a topic of interest at the college, yet few were taking the matter seriously.

While Bud and his friends were gathered one day at the campus café, they ran into Brett, whom they hadn't seen for a while. Brett had heard about their experiences with the wise man in the woods and he asked about them. One by one, they summarized what occurred in the tent. All of them were enthusiastic.

"You ought to go, Brett," said Agnes. "It's an experience that will change your life."

"Why does Brett need to go?" Steven intervened. "He's got every girl in the school in love with him."

"No wonder," said Molly, "He always looks so perfect. Those blue eyes, and the great clothes he always wears."

"Things may not be as good as they look," said Brett.

"What do you mean by that?" asked Bud.

"Perhaps it has been easier for me initially," Brett replied, "since my folks are well off. But in the long run, having everything handed to me on a silver platter may not have been so good for character building."

"What's wrong with your character?" inquired Molly.

"Well, because I was brought up to be a gentleman and taught to create good feelings with people, I'm predisposed to be agreeable," Brett explained. "Then, when I just go along with what other people dish out, I feel like I've given my power away."

"I don't know," said Marjorie, "I've seen you come back pretty strong to what some people have said."

"Sometimes people just see their side of things," Brett said, "and I feel that I have to show them that there are other ways of looking at the situation. It's not just the way they want it to be."

"It seems to me," Steven said, "that you wait too long to assert yourself until the other person has walked all over you, and then you feel you have to lash out and even the score. That's passive aggressive behavior according to what I've read. It's like you're waiting for a justification to vent your anger, and in some way you're setting up the confrontation."

"That's because they push my buttons!" Brett protested.

Bud stepped in. "Well, they're you're buttons, Brett, and they're under your control. Why allow other people to determine your course of action instead of calling the shots yourself?"

"I think that's what my problem is," said Brett. "If I don't have other people's approval, I feel powerless to act."

"If you want to resolve this," said Bud, "why don't I take you over to see Master Wiseheart? We all got a lot out of talking with him. I know he can help you as long as you are willing to speak your truth."

"OK. I'm sold. Let's go."

From Dependency to Respect

Master Wiseheart in his flowing green robe smiled with delight as Bud and Brett entered his tent. He fixed his gaze on the one he hadn't met before.

"Is there something that you wish to discuss with me, young man?"

Brett hesitated at first. He thought, 'All my life I've worried about how another person would react if I spoke candidly.' Brett then realized that his reluctance to speak his truth and possibly offend someone might be contributing to the issue he wanted to resolve. He now had an opportunity to overcome his reticence and speak up for himself.

"Everyone thinks I have the world by the tail," Brett began. "The truth is I am very dependent upon other people. My reactions to what they say and do seem to overpower my own initiative."

Bud interjected, "Why don't you try to function more independently, Brett?"

"I want to have someone to share my life with. I'd like a relationship with someone who respects me, someone who can motivate me. I don't do much when I'm alone."

"Brett, another person cannot make you what you are," said Master Wiseheart. "People go to great lengths to find someone who they think will turn their lives around. If your life is not working the way you would like it to, bringing in another person will only make the situation more complex and more difficult."

"Is it wrong for me to want a relationship because I believe it will make me happy?"

"No one can make you happy except you, Brett," said the Master.

"I think that if someone was my perfect complement they would bring out the best in me."

"The relationships you create serve as mirrors," the wise man said as he continued with his message. "They reflect back to you the truth about your essential nature."

"I want the reflection in the mirror to flatter me," Brett replied.

"To create the perfect partner, Brett, you would have to be the perfect partner. If you are unhappy with the way you are by yourself, there is no way being with someone else is going to make you happy."

"Does that mean that I will never find the right person?" Brett asked the Master.

"One does not find a relationship, one creates it. To find something implies that the resolution is outside you. A relationship needs to be born inside you first. Then the appropriate partner will show up who will serve your development at that time. When you open up a space inside yourself and actively participate in the process, you will realize that people are not doing anything *to* you, they are doing it *with* you. In that way you will be self-generating instead of a victim of circumstance."

"Why is it so difficult for me to find happiness in relationships?" asked Brett.

"Because you're looking for the relationship to give you something. An important key to success in a relationship is to enter it from a place of sharing rather than getting. Instead of coming from need, my young friend, start coming from love. Then you won't grow angry when other people don't accommodate your expectations. You will enjoy relating far more once you take responsibility for your own happiness."

Then Master Wiseheart proceeded to say something that seemed to sail over the heads of his visitors.

"The ultimate truth is that there is only one person here. Each one of us is a part of the Great Love, the creative life force. When we all expand into a more inclusive consciousness that honors this reality, then we will be able to move away from feelings of dependence and enter any kind of relationship feeling whole and complete."

"That's a radical idea!" Brett said. "I don't know if I could see everyone as one person."

"It's not something you see, Brett, it's something you feel when you reconnect with the Great Love. Let me give you an affirmation that will support you in making this shift in consciousness. It's a powerful phrase for you to repeat aloud several times a day, especially whenever you're looking to get something from another person. Please write this down."

> **Every relationship offers me
> an opportunity to express
> the Great Love that I am.**

"I see that this reverses my outlook from 'what can people give me?' to 'who can I be in their presence?' Thank you, Master Wiseheart, for your sage advice. And thanks to you, Bud. Our session here today has given me a lot to ponder."

Then just as Brett and Bud were about to leave, Brett turned to the Master and spoke to him one more time. "You know," he said, "I was just thinking. I would like to bring this girl I'm currently dating over to see you, Master."

"You mean Aurora?" asked Bud.

"Yes. We have some issues together that I'd like to discuss."

"You are welcome to visit anytime," said the Master graciously.

"Oh, we'll be back in no time," Brett said. "Life is becoming clearer by the minute."

LESSON EIGHT

AURORA – "I need to be fulfilled"

"Hello, Master Wiseheart, I'm Aurora."

There she stood, the most voluptuous girl on campus, the object of many a young man's erotic fantasy. Aurora was the embodiment of heart-stopping sensuality. Her thick dark hair framed a gorgeous coffee-colored complexion. Her penetrating eyes enhanced by luxuriously long lashes suggested a quality that was both mysterious and seductive. If Helen of Troy launched a thousand ships, Aurora left a wake of a thousand broken hearts.

"Welcome, Aurora," said the Master. "You are Brett's friend, are you not?"

"Well, we're more than friends. We've been dating for five months now."

"Did Brett not come with you?"

"Oh yes, he's here. He's waiting in the car. I wanted some private time with you."

"Is there something troubling you?"

"Master Wiseheart, I've been troubled all my life, only I have never admitted it. I don't want people to know what's going on with me beneath the surface. I must confess, though, I do want to see inside them."

"Why do you feel you have to cover up what is true?" the Master asked.

"I don't want anyone to take advantage of me, so I put on a brave, tough front that sends out a message."

"What's the message that you're sending out, Aurora?"

"Don't mess with me...or else! Mostly it's a bluff. It usually works though. I always win."

"What is it that you win?"

"I win the match. It's them against me. I know how to gain the advantage so that I don't turn out to be the victim."

"Why not simply declare that you're not a victim, Aurora?" suggested the Master. "No one can turn you into a victim if you do not see yourself as one. It appears as if you're setting up every interaction as a contest where someone has to lose."

Aurora looked at the wise man wearing a long burgundy-colored robe and sitting quietly in front of a large candle. She perceived in his eyes the enormous depth of his soul.

"Well, I do see the other person as someone who might take something away from me. I want to make sure that doesn't happen."

"When you give freely of yourself, nothing is taken away from you. Instead, you become more of what you can be. You'll begin to realize that every relationship offers you an opportunity to discover more of who you are. Then you'll see other people in a new light and you'll feel differently toward them."

"I always thought my feelings were beyond my control. You seem to be saying they're not."

The Master shook his head to indicate to Aurora that her feelings were not beyond her control.

Aurora began to pour out the contents of her heart. "I cannot seem to find enough in life to bring me any kind of lasting satisfaction. What happens is that I fall back on nasty habits—promiscuous sex, intoxicants and other forms of licentious behavior."

"It sounds as if your choices are substitutes for genuine fulfillment."

"A lot of times I just can't stop myself. I've had experiences in my life that felt so exquisitely beautiful and so rich. They have sent me soaring to heights I don't think a lot of people get to reach. My emotions run to extremes and my likes and dislikes acquire such intensity that they seem irreversible. I've been to what people call heaven and I've been to what they call hell. Either something is great for me, or it's terrible—worse than terrible."

"What is the value of being this way?"

"I love it!" said Aurora. "Brett is so middle-of-the-road, that's why I'm having a problem with our relationship. It's just not fulfilling enough for me. I want a relationship that takes me to my outer limits and my innermost depths—the highest and the lowest levels of my consciousness. Brett says I'm insatiable! I want to experience a rush when I'm with someone—get all the juices in my system flowing. I want to feel charged up and alive."

Then Aurora's spirit deflated. "Sometimes though, I feel as if I'm dying."

"Tell me Aurora, does anything fulfill you?"

"Sex does. Oh, not the physical part so much. But something happens in a sexually intimate situation when I'm with a partner who matches my intensity."

"So you do experience satisfaction through your relationships?"

"I have in the past, Master Wiseheart, but not right now. Not with Brett. He's too in control of his feelings, in an almost mechanistic way. I hardly ever see him experience raw emotion—and that's what I need. Brett's afraid to confront his darker feelings. For me, though, that's part of being human."

"What are these feelings that you label dark?"

"Oh, you know. It's the feelings I have that become uncomfortable after a while, like jealousy and feeling deeply resentful toward someone. These are feelings that are hard to deal with. Still, they move me in a new direction. They're painful, but they're transformational."

"How are they transformational?"

"When I feel the pain of my experience reaching a crescendo, then I have to do something about it."

"What do you do when that happens?"

"I release. I let go for good. I change."

"Aurora, it seems you have done a great deal of soul searching."

"I have. I'm very interested in exploring myself and going deeply into life. I'm a psych major at school."

"Yes," said the Master, nodding that he was not surprised.

"I spend a lot of time by myself," Aurora added.

"Are you avoiding people?" the Master asked.

"I seem to want more from them than they are willing to give me. I hold back, so they do too. I thought if I first got what I wanted, then I would be willing to give what I have. It doesn't seem to work that way though."

"No, it does not," said the Master. "Still, a lot of people believe that it does. Many of us are carrying around painful memories from an unsatisfied childhood. We desire to rewrite our personal histories by creating a partner who is going to give us everything we want. We may never actually ask for these things, yet we somehow expect them, and grow cold and indifferent when they are not forthcoming."

From Insatiability to Passion

"Is there a way to gain true satisfaction?" Aurora asked the Master.

"The key to gaining satisfaction is to take care of your soul. The soul has great knowledge and deep insight, yet this is held in secret, Aurora, until you realize that you are a channel for universal intelligence."

"What happens then?" asked Aurora.

"You acknowledge that your life is valuable and that it merits the greatest of efforts to make yourself as strong as possible. But you do not have to be hard to stay strong. The added strength you acquire comes from the passion within your soul that has learned over eons of time how to survive on the earth. In your willingness to be uncomfortable and accept many changes in your life, you tap into the very powers that have enabled your soul to prevail."

"Are you talking about other lives, Master?"

"You might see it that way, if you choose. Your soul, however, does not experience past existences the way your ego would perceive them. To your ego, the past is as personal as the present. To the soul, the past continues on in everyone. Thus, it belongs to everyone and not anyone in particular. The soul's concern is moving ahead of the past and developing a contribution that can, in some way, become a valuable part of the future."

"Well if it's not personal, in what way does the soul continue on?"

"The soul is a legacy of unfulfilled wishes, and the people who are alive now inherit those wishes and continue the efforts to bring them into manifestation."

"Wow! That's a really cool way of looking at the idea of past lives. What can I do to be a part of manifesting this legacy?"

"You can tap into the Great Love, that part of you at the core of your being that is one with the universe and at peace with everything in it. When you silence the ego-mind, you can hear your soul's longing."

Just then there was a noise. Aurora and the Master both looked up and saw Brett standing there. "I'm sorry to intrude," he said. "You have been in here for a while, Aurora, and you know I don't like to be alone."

"It's fine, Brett. Come sit down and join us. Master Wiseheart has been helping me a lot. I am glad you came in because there is one other issue I wanted to talk about and it has to do with you."

"What is it?" Brett asked, his curiosity switching to apprehension when he saw the look on her face.

"I just don't think you and I are going to make it."

"Why not?"

"I don't experience the passion that I want in our relationship. It feels so bland, as if you are trying to keep everything on an even keel when what I want is intensity and excitement. I had that when I was dating Bud, but he never sticks with anything. It was great at the start and then it fizzled out very quickly. You, Brett, are more dependable perhaps, though I think it is because you are so dependent."

"What are we going to do, Aurora?" asked Brett.

"I don't know about you, Brett. I'm learning that the power to change my life is in my hands."

"And the power to change my life is in mine," said Brett, speaking with a newfound clarity.

"Aurora," said the Master, "Perhaps you have expected that your life would be emotionally richer if your partner was willing to give more. Instead, know that the source of passion is in you. Of course, it all depends on where you direct your passionate energy—into your lower depths or into your higher self."

"But I don't want to choose between those two," Aurora said. "I don't want to give up any part of me."

"Emphasize the part of you that makes you feel good about yourself, the part of you that is evolving toward wholeness, not fragmentation. This is how you rise above your inner conflicts so that you can put all your energy into becoming the person you want to be. The more you practice self-control, the more you will be able to handle your energies without damage. Then you will see the value of discipline and you will know that it is worth it."

"I guess if I have been insatiable in the past, it is because I haven't asked the best of myself."

"I have a special phrase for you that will help remind you," said the Master. "Repeat it often throughout the day so you will remember it at those times when you feel you're losing control. Please write this down."

> **I embrace every part of myself
> as I listen to the longing of my soul
> and move toward my highest purpose.**

Slowly Aurora and Brett got up from the floor of the tent, thanked Master Wiseheart and made their exit. As they left Aurora said to Brett, "I don't think anything will ever be the same after tonight."

LESSON NINE

LANCE – "I need to be right"

Brett was glum as he drove Aurora home. When they reached her house, he turned to her just as she was about to get out of the car. "I want to ask you something," he said.

"What is it?"

"I heard that you were dating someone else. I heard it was this guy named Lance."

"It's true, I am. You don't know him, Brett. He's not at the school. He used to be, but he dropped out and started traveling around the world. He wanted a hands-on experience of life. He told me that he learned more from his travels than he did from any class lecture."

"I heard he was cool," said Brett. "Bud knows him and Max knows him real well."

"Lance may come back to school in the fall," Aurora continued. "He wants a degree. Right now, he's not doing too much. He says he's looking for direction, he's searching for a purpose."

"Remember what the Master told Bud and Molly about love giving us the power to manifest whatever supports our purpose?"

"Yeah. Let's go see Lance and tell him about Master Wiseheart."

Brett was a bit hesitant.

"Don't worry Brett," Aurora assured him. "Lance is not the jealous type."

"I'm working at not being jealous either," said Brett.

Even though it was late, Brett and Aurora went over to Lance's apartment that same evening.

Aurora opened up the discussion. "Lance," she said, "have you heard about the wise man in the woods who's giving advice? He's incredible! He has the most amazing insights to share."

"Oh yeah, that wizard. I heard about him. What's his name again?"

"Master Wiseheart," volunteered Brett.

"You were talking about searching for purpose in your life," Aurora said, "and that you're in a transition period right now. I really think you should go see this man. It's the best thing you could do."

"How do you arrange a meeting with him?" asked Lance. "Make an appointment or something?"

"No," said Aurora, "you just show up and be fully present. That would be a kind of a novelty for you, Lance."

Lance did a double take and then looked at Brett. "Aurora thinks my head is in the clouds."

"I could think of worse places for your head to be," Brett said with an impish grin on his face.

"You know, Lance," Aurora said, "Master Wiseheart has a very deep understanding of life. I just know he could help point you in the right direction."

"OK, that's it. I want to see this guy immediately," Lance declared.

"You mean now?" Brett asked.

"If you're that eager," said Aurora, "let's hop in the car and go over there right now."

From Arrogance to Wisdom

Master Wiseheart was in a deep meditative trance when Brett and Aurora brought Lance to see him. Aurora was surprised that the Master was now wearing a luminous blue robe. She noticed that the whole tent seemed to pick up the tinge of it.

"It's so beautiful in here," said Aurora. "Master Wiseheart, this is my friend, Lance. He wanted to meet you."

"He is the next in line," said the Master.

"What do you mean by that?" asked Lance.

"Students often speak about these visits," said the Master. "Still, only certain people actually come. What can I do for you tonight, Lance?"

"I've been traveling, Master Wiseheart," said Lance. "Now I think I'm ready to return to my home town and take on responsibilities. Another part of me, though, still wants adventure, still wants to keep traveling. It's kind of a conflict that I can't resolve."

"Have you asked for anyone else's advice about this matter?" asked the Master.

A quizzical look came over Lance's face. He wondered why the sage would ask him that particular question. "No," Lance said. "I rarely take advice from anyone. I don't appreciate being told that I'm wrong. I hate to be in doubt."

"Why do you have doubts?" the Master asked Lance.

"Because some of the ideas I call my own I really just got from books or other people. That's why I decided to go out and see the world. I wanted to discover my own truth."

"And what did you find, Lance, out there in the world?" asked the Master.

"People with different points of view, ones that contradicted mine in many cases. At first I argued with them, blindly trying to defend the adopted ideas that made up my philosophy. Later I realized that there are many different ways of looking at life that are equally valid."

"That troubled you, didn't it, Lance?" Aurora inquired.

"Yes, it did," said Lance. "I wanted to live in a black and white world where the truth was absolute. Instead I found myself in a gray world where few things seemed incontestable."

"Natural laws are incontestable," the Master said with certainty.

"You mean," said Lance, "things everybody knows, like gravity and electromagnetism? I'm not talking about the physical world. I'm talking about the less tangible issues in life, the things that I still have serious doubts about. I don't want to go along with what everybody else believes, because they could be wrong. I need to be right! That's my issue."

"Why not see if we can reframe this?" the Master suggested. "Think of it, Lance. When you need to be right, it implies that someone else must be wrong. You will end up inflating your ego at the expense of others. There is no happiness in that. Would you rather be right than happy?"

"I'd rather know the truth," said Lance.

"There are many possible truths," replied the Master. "It is arrogant to think that any piece of the truth one has realized is the whole and unchanging truth. A mind that refuses to consider that the evolving world is asking for further illumination is neither supporting the advancement of human consciousness nor allowing for the opportunity of expanding possibilities."

Lance was growing restless. "Master, I am interested in knowing about things that are hidden from view."

"So am I," said Aurora. "You and I have that in common, Lance."

"Yes, we do," replied Lance. "Master Wiseheart, what is life? What is its secret, its mystery?"

Grinning from ear to ear, the Master looked first at Lance and then at Aurora and Brett. Then he spoke. "You want to know what's behind the mystery?"

"Yes, we do," they all said.

"The world is a testing ground for soul development," said Master Wiseheart.

"Do I graduate if I pass the test?" Lance asked.

"You graduate when you see that there is nothing wrong here."

"Wait a minute, Master Wiseheart," said Brett, who up to now had been sitting quietly in the background. "Sometimes things happen that are wrong."

"But they're not," replied the Master.

"They sure seem to be," Brett responded.

"What seems wrong to you, Brett, is your responsibility. If you don't like something, why blame that on the world?"

"You're not suggesting," said Brett, "that I'm responsible for everything that's wrong, are you?"

"No, because nothing is wrong—unless you say it is. If you keep saying it, it keeps getting worse until it becomes unbearable."

"What do you suggest we do?" Lance asked the Master.

"When something seems to be wrong, instead of taking the experience as a personal affront, choose to perceive it as an enriching learning experience. Everything is interconnected, Lance. Every single event that occurs in your life fits in with a larger pattern. You might consider the pattern a map of your entire existence."

"So what you're telling Lance is that there is a pattern to life," said Aurora. "The world does not operate simply by way of a random process. There is much more order to it than that."

"Yes," the Master concurred.

"Tell us more," said Lance. "It seems as if you know the secrets of the universe."

"The universe you live in," the Master said, "is fluid and creative. The energies that are moving through you, however, have a purposeful design. They are patterned so that your individual purpose can be fulfilled. You always have a choice. You can go with what flows most naturally, which is the Great Love inside you, or you can go off your path and against the current, attempting to force circumstances that you think are desirable. Regardless of what you choose, the universe limits how far your ego can go and how big it can become, and this is for your own good."

"That's hard to swallow," said Lance. "I don't want to accept that there are predetermined limits."

"No one can be whatever they want to be if it goes against what they intrinsically are. Each person has an agreement with the universe to contribute to the evolution of the planet, and if anyone attempts to move into spaces that go beyond their agreement, then the universe will apply constraints so as to not lose the balance of the whole."

"Well that's if I try to be something I'm not, but what if I honor what I am?" Lance asked.

"If you honor what you intrinsically are," Master Wiseheart answered, "the commitments you make to your truth are more important than what the world considers to be true. What you might have thought improbable before is now possible when you live out your convictions. Your reality is primarily a product of your thoughts and actions and, above all, a product of your love, which is part of the Great Love."

"Master Wiseheart, did the Great Love create the universe billions of years ago and then disappear from the scene?"

"Certainly not, Lance. The Great Love is still active both creating and experiencing itself through each one of us. This is how the creative force becomes increasingly aware of its nature. The creation grows bigger and greater with the ever-expanding multiplicity of beings and the things they produce."

"Does the Great Love watch over us and make note of everything we do? Does it reward or punish us accordingly?"

"No, Lance. The Great Love is not an external consciousness looking at us as objects. It is inside us looking out. We are the ones who punish or reward ourselves according to our own beliefs about what we deserve."

Then Lance asked the Master, "Did I choose my life or did it choose me?"

"What difference does it make? Your life is going to be what it is regardless of the answer to that question."

"Does that mean you don't know the answer?" Aurora probed, wondering if perhaps the wise teacher wasn't as wise as she thought.

"Aurora," the Master replied, "you are looking for absolutes in a world where there is only one."

"One? What is the one absolute?" she asked.

"Why, the Great Love, of course! Love is the one energy that will never die. It is both what creates life and what preserves it. Everything else—including all that you have perceived to be 'real'—is a transient illusion."

"You seem to be saying that there is no right or wrong, there is only choice." Lance said.

"Yes, and the choice to make is the one that honors who you intrinsically are—the Great Love, the only absolute truth."

"I just wish everybody knew this!" Lance said. "I want to go out there and spread the word."

"That would be proselytizing, which attempts to take away other people's free will. It would be arrogant for you to insist that others make the choice that you have made. Instead, be an example of the Great Love and allow people to see the living truth for themselves."

"But when I see people acting from a misguided view of life," said Lance, "I want to point out their error and show them a better way."

"People will not change because you want them to," the Master replied. "That's not enough motivation for them. You will do better to focus on how you want to change yourself. You see Lance, if you need to persuade someone else that you're right, then you really don't believe that you are. If you are confident in your truth, you don't need anyone else to agree with you. That is true wisdom."

"This sure is a different way of looking at things," Lance said.

"Let me give you an affirmation that will assist you to move in this direction. Repeat it aloud throughout the day, especially when you find yourself moving into judgment of others. Please write this down."

> **Through my words and deeds,**
> **I am a living example**
> **of what I believe to be true.**

"Well I can see that when I embody my true beliefs I am becoming an expression of the Great Love," said Lance. "Thank you Master. I am very pleased with what you have told us."

"It was my pleasure."

KATHERINE – "I need to prove myself"

Katherine knocked on the door of the yurt. The door opened and there stood the Master in a distinguished robe, which on this day was the color of charcoal.

"I'm Katherine," said the tall young lady with a stern expression.

Despite her somewhat severe demeanor, Katherine was a beautiful young woman, tall and sleek, with shoulder-length jet-black hair, deep blue eyes and high cheekbones.

"What can I do for you?" asked the wise man as he ushered his visitor to the center of the tent and graciously offered her a cushion. Katherine chose to remain standing.

"I'm not sure if you can do anything," said Katherine. "I heard about you from someone I know at college. I'm working on a degree there in business administration and have started a small business of my own. I came here because I was told you give expert advice. That is the only kind I am interested in."

"How may I advise you?" asked the Master.

"I don't know, Mr. Wiseheart, if you are a man of the world. The expert advice that I am looking for would have to come from someone who knows how the world works."

"What world are you referring to, Katherine?"

"The one we're in, of course!" Katherine retorted, a bit perturbed by the absurdity of the Master's question.

"There are many worlds, Katherine," the wise man answered calmly. "There is an infinite number of possible expressions of life. Reality is not cast in stone."

Katherine's response to this vision of chaos was immediate. "That sounds all over the map to me. I can't operate that way. I need to have everything organized."

"Being organized is an important skill," the Master agreed. "You could contribute greatly to many projects with that ability."

"That's good to hear," Katherine sighed, relieved that the mystic was not trying to get her to live in the woozy world he seemed to inhabit.

From Callousness to Integrity

"Why did you come here today?" the Master asked.

"I'm a very serious and ambitious person. Some people have accused me of being callous. I need to prove myself and I'm not about to let my emotions get in the way."

"So you'll stop at nothing to realize your ambitions?"

"Well, I am not willing to sell my soul to be successful. What I want is to build a good reputation."

"Katherine, a reputation is built by doing what you say you'll do and by meeting your responsibilities as capably as possible. When you are honest, self-disciplined and able to place your focus on the task at hand, then it can be seen by all that you have integrity."

"That is what I want—integrity," Katherine said and then paused for a moment. "You know, Master Wiseheart, from the time I was young, I was told to make something of myself. It was as if I had an adult mind in a young body. My father especially was very strict and I guess what you would call a pessimist. He would say harsh things to me as a child."

"What sort of things did he say?"

"He spoke of the hardships that I was bound to face as I tried to establish myself in the world. He said my worth as a human being would be decided by society and my being a female would only make achieving success more difficult. I think he was speaking from his own prejudices rather than from the truth."

"What is the truth, Katherine?" asked the Master.

"I thought you were the one that had all the answers, Wiseheart," Katherine blurted.

"I see," said the wise man. There was a long silence.

Sensing the Master was not going to speak until she did, Katherine attempted to answer the Master's question.

"I think the truth is that I need to be tough in order to reach my goals in a tough world. You know, the end justifies the means."

"I would prefer to say, Katherine, that the means ultimately decide the end."

Katherine did not want to take in the Master's comment, and she quickly changed the subject, or thought she did. "There's nothing wrong with wanting to have a significant impact upon the world, is there?" she asked.

"It all depends on how you do it," said the Master. "You are free to create or to destroy, to contribute or to cost."

"I wouldn't want to destroy anything. I want what I value to last forever."

"Sometimes it is necessary to put an end to something in order to make room for new growth. Nothing that is in this world is permanent."

Again Katherine shrugged off the Master's words. The conversation was not going where she wanted it to go.

The Master continued in spite of Katherine's indifference to his words of wisdom. "Many people have climbed the ladder of success, eager to claim the prize and prove their superiority. Often, however, they find that the most precious things are what they left behind. Having sacrificed what really matters— expressing the love that is inside them—they discover that success came at too high a price. They have competed and they've won, yet somewhere along the way they've lost touch with who they really are."

"Master Wiseheart, having a successful career is what matters to me, and love has no place in the business world." Katherine said.

"How do you intend to attract clients if you don't show concern for their well-being and treat them with kindness? You have to be nice to people if you want to succeed in business."

"First I want to make sure my business is successful and then I'll think about being nice to people."

"It doesn't work that way, Katherine."

"What do you mean? You don't understand. Nothing's going to prevent me from realizing my achievements."

"Loving is the greatest achievement," said the Master. "I'm not speaking of a desire-based love, I'm referring to the Great Love inside of you. That is the true source of your success, Katherine, not the outside world. You have a purpose to realize here and no one else can duplicate it."

"What would you say is my purpose?"

"The answer to that question does not come all at once, Katherine. It comes gradually as you put one foot in front of the other. After you complete each step, another clue shows up and allows you to move on to the next."

"That sounds too haphazard. I need to work with something more solid than that, something carefully thought out in advance."

"Succeeding in your career is not as hard as you seem to think. The most important thing is to love what you're doing, and then the world will appreciate your contribution because it comes from love."

"That's inspiring, but it's so different from what most people believe."

"What do you think most people believe?"

"That you have to put your personal feelings aside in business and sacrifice your desires for your career."

"No one has truly succeeded by dishonoring who they are," said the Master. "Always remain true to the Great Love in your heart and you will not be accused of being callous. Meet situations with humor so that your innate seriousness and ambition do not get too extreme and obscure your true purpose."

"I always thought my purpose was to be successful in business and that I needed to carefully plan so that success was inevitable. Now you're telling me that it's more about love and humor and I don't know how to fit that in with my agenda."

"That's because you're working with preconceptions instead of allowing your life to flow spontaneously. Let me give you an affirmation that will help you. Repeat it aloud throughout the day, and especially whenever you feel stuck. Please write this down."

> **My purpose becomes clear
> as I move beyond preconceptions
> and respond to the present with love.**

"I want to thank you, Master Wiseheart. A lot of people are talking about you and now I see why. You are indeed a sage!"

"Remember one more thing, Katherine."

"What is that?"

"It takes one to know one," he said with a wink.

LESSON ELEVEN

MORGAN – "I need to be different"

Katherine had given her friend Morgan directions to Master Wiseheart's tent. When he got to the place she had described he saw the large round tent in the woods. Bud told him that you just walk in, so he did.

There, in the center of the round room, was a funny little bald man in a purple robe. Morgan thought to himself, 'this guy's part wizard and part monk.'

"Hello, young man. What brings you here to see me?" the sage asked.

"Hi. My name's Morgan. Actually my friend Katherine told me about you and I wanted to check you out and see if I agree with the things you have to say."

"What if you don't agree with what I have to say?"

"That will make me more sure of what I already know."

"Morgan, is there something you'd like to discuss?"

"Well, I'd like to talk about what's going on in the world today. It sure seems to me that we're heading into some strange times. Don't you think that's true?"

"To me, nothing is strange."

"What I'm talking about is the dishonesty and cynicism in society. I'd like to see more people in high places who care about the greater good and not just filling up their own pockets. Our institutions are crumbling, corruption is widespread, and most people feel powerless to make things better."

"What are you personally doing about this?" Master Wiseheart asked.

"A lot, actually. I'm involved in several organizations that are doing different things to bring about progress. We're working toward a more equitable society. You see, I'm really a revolutionary out to change the world."

"You've taken on a big project—changing the world."

"Oh, don't get me wrong" said Morgan. "It's not that I have all the answers or feel that I'm better than anyone else. I just think that our society could use an upgrade and I'm willing to fight for that."

"Do you really mean 'fight'?"

"Yeah! We went out on the streets and protested the war. We were a million people strong. We made a lot of noise and really shook up the system."

"It sounds like you created another war," said the Master. "Isn't that fighting fire with fire?"

"Sometimes things are so wrong that you have to stand up to the forces that are upsetting the balance. Throughout history people have fought against injustices and succeeded in bringing about positive changes in the world."

"Instead of protesting aggressively, don't you think you could be more effective in bringing about change by setting a peaceful example?"

"It would be hard to find many instances in human history where that has happened."

From Rebelliousness to Freedom

"Morgan," said the Master, "is that the highest we can achieve—to keep fighting—or could we eventually reach a place where that wouldn't be necessary any more? If you oppose something you make it stronger by giving it more energy. You could use that energy to rise to another level and build the new rather than tear down the old."

"Oh I'm with you, wise man! I've got one foot in the real world and one foot in a new world. And that's part of my dilemma. There's such a big discrepancy between the way I know the world could be and the way the world is."

"What is your concept of how the world could be?" the Master asked.

"It's a world where everyone is on an equal footing and no one is being exploited. It's a society where the greater good takes precedence over selfish interests. Perhaps it's idealistic, but I think it's the only way for people to be genuinely happy."

"Morgan, the way the world is demonstrates what is humanly possible as of now. Perhaps the world can become the way you feel it should, but only if you and others become that way yourselves. Change yourself, Morgan. Raise the vibrations around you and draw a higher quality of experience into your life. That is your best shot at changing the world."

"I don't see how that changes the world, Master Wiseheart. That just improves my life and maybe a few people's lives around me. I want to move more quickly than that."

"Believe it or not, the fastest way to bring about the changes you seek is one person at a time, one by one by one. Successful reforms are more like a grassfire than a conflagration. When change comes in this way, it may seem slow at first, but at a certain point it reaches critical mass and becomes global."

"That's what I want to do!" said Morgan. "I want to bring about global change. I want to work in community with others. The only thing is, I don't like anyone pressuring me to conform to their ways."

"But when you're protesting, aren't you trying to get other people to conform to your way of thinking?"

"No, the groups I'm working with are giving them a choice, an opportunity to embrace change. We're not coercing or manipulating them in any way. Although I have to admit, I feel a little bit coerced and manipulated by the people in my groups."

"Why is that?" asked the Master.

"When I'm in a group I have to be cooperative and I feel a natural resistance to giving up my autonomy."

"Did it occur to you, Morgan," asked the Master, "that the group that is inviting you to participate might be burned out on its own particular story and is yearning for a breath of fresh air that they feel you could provide?"

"I'd like to think that's possible," Morgan said. "You know, I used to be afraid that unless I became a team player I would be ostracized. I thought I had to be that nonentity I call 'John Q. Public.' You know, he's the guy the marketing people are trying to sell. He's just an ordinary human being giving his attention to the popular culture. I couldn't do it though. I've struggled with this because I always needed to be different."

"You don't need anything, Morgan."

"What I mean is that I want to open up my life to innovation so that electrifying changes can take place."

"You are close to it!" the Master said. "Take the freedom to express your true self in the world and encourage each person you know to do the same. Be confident that your friends love you for who you are and love them back for who they are. That is the secret to getting along with people."

"Oh I like people all right," Morgan continued, perhaps not registering the full impact of what was just said, "And I would like them to like me. I just don't want their expectations to overrule my own choices. I would like freedom and responsibility to carry equal weight in my life. The moment I can no longer support the group vision, I'll take the nearest exit."

"Morgan," said the Master. "You are a peerless expression of love and your energy will always be welcome in the human community. You already understand that the differences between people are enriching rather than threatening. You know that if one feels threatened, it is a purely subjective experience that has nothing to do with other people. Don't hold yourself back in deference to their fears. Show them how you shine your light and their fears will start to evaporate."

"Thank you, Master Wiseheart," Morgan said, finally getting it. "I am inspired by your observations and the wisdom you share. You have helped me to see that I can be loved because of my uniqueness, not in spite of it. There is tremendous freedom in that, and that is the way I wish to be loved."

"Yes, Morgan, and because you know your own heart, you will be contributing to the manifestation of the collective heartbeat." Master Wiseheart was beaming at his newest prodigy. "As you participate in a group effort in this new way, your sense of identity will shift from your shrinking ego-self to your expanding universal self. Then you will be glad that you traded in your ego's need to be important in exchange for a life rich in human contact and a shared sense of identity."

Morgan was beaming, too. He had never felt so free of internal conflict. "Everything you say makes a lot of sense to me. It's not common knowledge, but it's actually common sense."

"Once you go deeply into the truth, what you discover seems so obvious. Let me send you on your way with an affirmation, a phrase that will remind you of what we talked about today. Repeat it often, especially whenever you feel a rebellious urge. Please write this down."

> **I am only as free
> as I allow everyone else to be.**

As Morgan rose from the floor to leave, he said, "Tomorrow, we're all coming back here. "

"Who is coming here tomorrow?" the Master asked.

"All of us from the college who have met with you in the past couple of weeks. You know: Bud, Molly, Steven, Marjorie, Max, Agnes, Brett, Aurora, Lance, Katherine and me. We all know each other and have been talking about our visits with you. Anyway someone new is coming. Her name is Crystal. We can't wait to hear what you have to say to her. So we're all coming to see you tomorrow."

"Well, we'll see. Good night, Morgan."

"Good night, Master Wiseheart, and thank you."

LESSON TWELVE

CRYSTAL – "I need to be happy"

The next evening, at the time agreed, Bud and his friends met outside the yurt. They had all been through the experience of meeting with the wise and loving teacher who taught them about the Great Love and they were eager to meet with the Master once again.

Crystal was the only person who had not yet arrived. She had been out of town.

"Where did Crystal go on her trip?" Molly asked Agnes.

"She never told me where she was going, just that she would be gone for a while and not reachable by phone," responded Agnes. "She finally called me when she came home last night. I told her about our special meeting with Master Wiseheart tonight, and she said she wanted to come but would be a little late."

Since it was getting cold out, they decided they would all go inside, and Crystal would know she was to join them when she arrived. Bud opened the door. It was darker than usual, with just one large candle burning softly in the center of the room, where the Master always sat in the lotus position.

"Where is Master Wiseheart?" Bud asked.

"Look, on the floor!" said Katherine.

"The Master is on the floor?" Marjorie said in a startled voice.

"No," said Katherine. "Here are his robes, all laid out in a circle. Each robe is a different color. There is the charcoal robe he wore when I went to see him."

"He wore red the first time I came," said Bud. "Then his robe was brown when I brought Molly."

"He wore an Orange robe when I was here," Steven said.

"There's my silver robe," said Marjorie.

"He was wearing a yellow robe when I met him," said Max.

"Look," said Agnes, "I see the beige robe he wore when I was here."

"He wore a green robe the day I went to see him," said Brett.

"Burgundy on mine," said Aurora.

"So it looks as if he greeted each of us with a different robe," said Morgan. "His robe was purple when I was here, which happens to be my favorite color."

Then Brett commented, "The robes are the same style though, no matter what the color."

Then Katherine offered this idea. "It's likely that the robe the Master wore the day of our visit indicates the place for each of us to stand while we wait for him. I'll stand by the charcoal robe."

"I think we are supposed to wear these robes," said Steven.

"I think we are too," Lance said confidently. "Look, the blue robe has a tag with my name on it."

"Mine too," said Agnes.

So each member of the group put on the robe apparently assigned to them, and stood in their places in a circle around the candle. When they did this, something amazing occurred. All of a sudden the energy seemed to become more focused and the light intensified. When the group had entered the tent it was fairly dark. Now it seemed to the members of the group that the inside of the yurt was becoming lighter and everything looked so much clearer, although no one had an explanation for why this was so.

Then, without making a sound, Crystal entered the tent dressed in a multicolored robe. She looked absolutely radiant, just like a princess, with her long black hair and milky white skin. Everyone excitedly greeted her and brought her into the circle.

"Where have you been, Crystal?" asked Bud.

"Oh, I'm not sure you would believe me," Crystal replied, appearing to Bud as if she were uncomfortable with his question.

"Master Wiseheart is not here, at least not in body," said Steven.

"It feels as if he's here in spirit," Aurora said convincingly.

"Since all of us obviously believe in him, it is fair to say that he is here in spirit," Crystal said softly.

No one was about to discount Crystal's remark because they knew she was a gifted intuitive who was able to receive information most people could not pick up.

After a long pause, Lance broke the silence. "What do you mean when you say the Master is here in spirit?"

"You asked me where I've been," said Crystal. "Well, I've been to another frequency. I discovered a new world even though I never left this one. The sense of my physical self began dissolving while the intensity of the light deep within me became stronger. It was as if the physical dimension was disappearing and I realized that everything was energetically connected. I now see everything in a different light and I believe the Master is an illusion."

"You mean he never existed?" said Katherine. "I find that hard to believe."

"An illusion is when you think you see something that isn't really there," replied Crystal. "You saw an illusion; however that certainly does not mean that you saw nothing. It's just that you didn't see what you thought."

"Then it was a collective hallucination," said Morgan. "We all saw one thing and experienced something else, is that what you are saying, Crystal?"

Crystal paused for a moment and then suggested to her peers, "Let's do a quick exercise and I think you will begin to understand." Crystal closed her eyes and began to speak, yet somehow her voice had completely changed.

"Now that you have on the Master's robes, walk around greeting one another. What do you see as you look into each other's eyes?"

The group members walked about the room. They gazed into each other's eyes. They looked into the windows of each other's soul and they all saw the same thing: the deep and penetrating yet kindly and nurturing eyes of Master Wiseheart.

Everyone was speechless. 'Was it really true?' they all wondered. 'Was Master Wiseheart an illusion, a figment of each person's imagination that they wanted to believe in so much that it seemed to happen? Was it real or was it a waking dream? Could all twelve individuals have the same dream?'

Needless to say, everyone in the room, except Crystal, was mystified. Therefore, the group looked to her to clear up the confusion.

"One thing we all notice right away," said Crystal. "Master Wiseheart is not physically present, yet we sense his presence."

"That's true," said Marjorie.

"He was here physically every other time one of us came to see him," said Morgan.

"Now he's gone," said Aurora. "Gone for good."

"No," said Crystal. "He is as much here now as he ever was. I have a story to tell you about myself and I think it will help you to further make sense of what happened."

"Good," said Katherine. "I hate to be in the dark."

From Escapism to Transcendence

Crystal started sharing her story. "About a month ago I had reached the end of the line and was at the end of my rope. I felt disconnected from the world and life seemed meaningless to me. Everything I did was a vain search for happiness that left me feeling lonely and lost. I sank into a state of apathy, paralyzed by so many defeats and unwilling to pick myself up and make another effort. 'What's the use?' I thought. My dreams were not coming true. I had drunk the nectar from many cups, yet all I could feel was deep disappointment. I wanted to escape any way I could."

Crystal looked around the circle at her absorbed audience. Then she said, "That is when I created Master Wiseheart."

"You CREATED him? A flesh and blood person!" exclaimed Steven, whose logical mind was jarred by Crystal's off-the-wall assertion.

"I created him because I am him," said Crystal. "The group was able to see the Master just a minute ago when we all looked into each other's eyes because each of us is the Master. He is a composite projection of the love and wisdom in our hearts. Only we could not accept the responsibility of having all of this love and wisdom. So each one of us projected these qualities onto our image of a master teacher. What we thought was his is really ours, but we were not comfortable with claiming it for ourselves. So we denied that part of our being that already knows the truth. We gave our light to him, so that he could be the embodiment of the good in us while we still had the liberty to go out, have fun and behave outrageously."

"It doesn't seem that you did that, Crystal," said Agnes.

"No. I always knew that there was great wisdom and understanding in my heart. I knew that I had powers that I had hardly tapped into and that I was barely scratching the surface of who I was. Then I heard his voice, the Master Wiseheart inside me, and the voice became so clear that I was able to project an image of a face and body to go along with it. Astonishing as it may sound, my idealized projection appeared as a real flesh and blood person. Of course, it wasn't flesh and blood. It seemed that way to all of us here because it was the only way we could remain in denial about who we really are."

"Has all of this been a set-up, Crystal? Did you plan all of this?" asked Katherine.

"I simply want people to know who they are," Crystal said unapologetically, "and to realize that they are not alone. We are all united in the energy of love."

Molly felt disconnected from the conversation and said to Crystal. "That's all well and good, but could we talk about *real* things?"

"Molly," said Crystal, "I learned that it is possible to project a real live image that would communicate that we are all connected to the same source of light. I thought no one would ever listen to me, so I had to create someone they could not argue with—someone infinitely wise and absolutely perfect. Then I started telling a few people about the amazing Master Wiseheart and his words of wisdom."

"Yes," said Bud, "I was the first who came to see him in this tent and the rest of you followed."

"When each of you went to see the Master," Crystal continued, "he was real to you because you so much wanted him to be."

"But the Master had the answers for us," Steven said.

"The truth is, we are the ones who have the answers to our prayers locked in our hearts."

"That is what the Master told me," said Marjorie. "If I want something in my life, I have to want it to be true and with all my heart I have to believe that it can be true."

"I'm still finding this story hard to swallow," said Steven. "I mean I saw the guy. He was short and his head was shaven and…"

"No, Steven, Master Wiseheart had dark, curly hair and a Buddha belly," said Katherine.

"No, he was tall and slender and had long, golden hair," said Lance.

"You see what's happening?" said Crystal. "You each perceived a different illusion. It was based on the powerful preconception you had of what the Master would be like even before you met him. That preconception was a thought form that materialized into what appeared to be a person, when it was actually a product of your creative imagination."

"Crystal," said Max, "what was your experience of being in the presence of this thought form that had materialized into an embodiment of your wishful thinking?"

"As I said, it has changed my life and taken me to a new level of consciousness. Now I see the magic in every moment of existence. I hear my inner voice telling me to let go of any barrier that obscures the light emanating from me."

"How do you do this, Crystal?" Max wanted to know. "How do you rise to these higher levels?"

"First of all," said Crystal, "I let go of any belief that says I cannot reach them. Then I hear my inner voice. It tells me to stand in the light and be informed and healed by the light. It tells me that what I am experiencing is my own creation and not to quarrel with it. It is then that I understand that I am completely accountable for my experience and that everything is unfolding exactly as it should. No matter how hard things may seem, I keep learning to trust that love is present."

"Don't you have any fears, Crystal?" asked Aurora.

"Nothing else is present except love, so there is nothing to fear. Love is the brightest light, the most enduring energy and the ultimate truth. Love is what makes an illusion real."

"Love is what made Master Wiseheart real," said Agnes. "You were right Max, believing is seeing."

"The Master," said Crystal, "the wise being that lives in me, taught me that I will never be happy if I need to be. If instead, I graciously receive the experiences that come to me, and if I realize they are the inevitable outcome of what I have contributed through my thoughts and my deeds, then I can experience the serenity of inner peace."

There was absolute silence in the tent. Everyone was profoundly moved by Crystal's words, and there was undeniably much more light in the tent than there had been when they entered it.

Crystal continued. "This, I believe, is what happiness ultimately is. It is the ability to bring into my life a gift of grace, a valuable experience that will teach me something I am choosing to learn. Happiness is even better than I thought it was."

"Crystal," Morgan said, "we all got affirmations from the Master. What is yours?"

Crystal closed her eyes as was her habit when repeating her affirmation.

> **I now embrace whatever shows up for me, and the world embraces me in return.**

The friends in the circle put their arms on each other's shoulders and looked into each other's eyes. Once again they saw in each other the eyes of the Master. They saw in each radiant face their own highest self. The twelve then just stood in silence, their arms solidifying the circle. It was getting noticeably lighter and lighter in the tent. The light intensified so much that they all simultaneously closed their eyes for an instant. When they opened their eyes, the tent was gone, and they were standing outside under the stars. They looked up and saw themselves a million times over in the heavens.

Without a word, they disbanded and went to their cars, not knowing if they would ever stop smiling.